GERALD COBB
MVO, FSA

London City Churches

B.T. Batsford Ltd
London

First published 1942
New and revised edition published 1977
© Gerald Cobb 1977
ISBN 0 7134 3186 5

Filmset in 10 on 12pt. Garamond by
Servis Filmsetting Ltd, Manchester
Designed by Lloyd Martin
Printed and bound in Great Britain by
The Anchor Press Ltd, Tiptree, Essex
for the publishers
B.T. Batsford Ltd, 4 Fitzhardinge Street,
London W1H 0AH

Charles & Barbara Gregersen

June 15, 1984

LONDON CITY CHURCHES

1 London from Islington church tower 1789, from an engraving by John Swertner

Contents

Illustrations

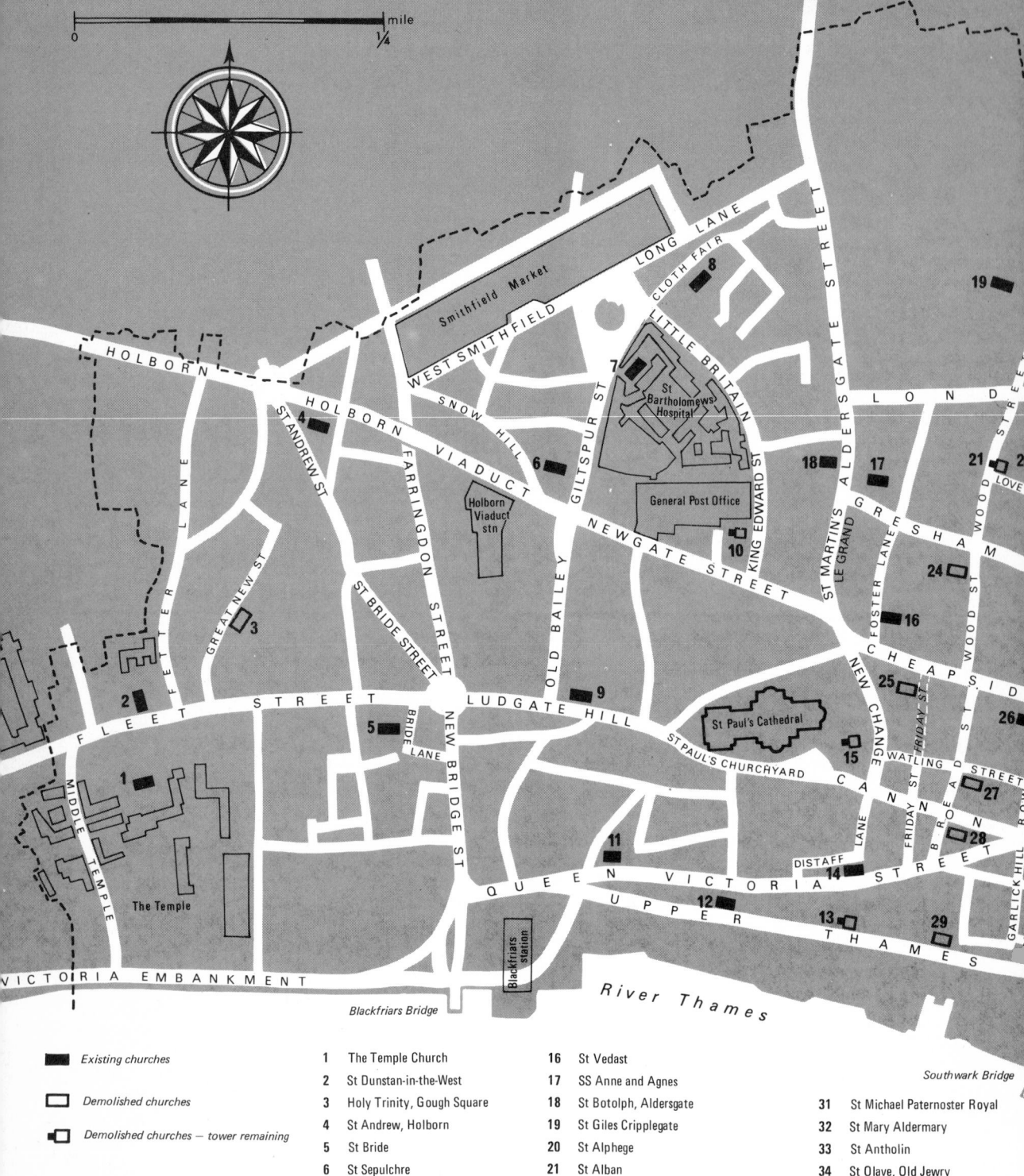

	mile
0	¼

Smithfield Market

WEST SMITHFIELD

SNOW HILL

HOLBORN

HOLBORN VIADUCT

Holborn Viaduct stn

ST ANDREW ST

GREAT NEW ST

FARRINGDON STREET

ST BRIDE STREET

BRIDE LANE

NEW BRIDGE ST

FETTER LANE

FLEET STREET

MIDDLE TEMPLE

The Temple

VICTORIA EMBANKMENT

Blackfriars Bridge

LUDGATE HILL

OLD BAILEY

NEWGATE STREET

GILTSPUR ST

CLOTH FAIR

LONG LANE

LITTLE BRITAIN

St Bartholomews Hospital

KING EDWARD ST

General Post Office

ST MARTIN'S LE GRAND

ALDERSGATE STREET

FOSTER LANE

LOND...

GRESHAM

WOOD ST

LOVE

CHEAPSID...

St Paul's Cathedral

ST PAUL'S CHURCHYARD

NEW CHANGE

CANN...

DISTAFF LANE

WATLING ST

FRIDAY ST

BREAD ST

FRIDAY ST

QUEEN VICTORIA STREET

UPPER THAMES

Blackfriars station

CANNON STREET

BOW LANE

GARLICK HILL

River Thames

Southwark Bridge

Existing churches

Demolished churches

Demolished churches — tower remaining

- - - - - Boundary of the City of London

1 The Temple Church
2 St Dunstan-in-the-West
3 Holy Trinity, Gough Square
4 St Andrew, Holborn
5 St Bride
6 St Sepulchre
7 St Bartholomew-the-Less
8 St Bartholomew-the-Great
9 St Martin Ludgate
10 Christ Church, Newgate Street
11 St Andrew-by-the-Wardrobe
12 St Benet Paul's Wharf
13 St Mary Somerset
14 St Nicholas Cole Abbey
15 St Augustine

16 St Vedast
17 SS Anne and Agnes
18 St Botolph, Aldersgate
19 St Giles Cripplegate
20 St Alphege
21 St Alban
22 St Mary Aldermanbury *(Foundations only)*
23 St Michael Bassishaw
24 St Michael, Wood Street
25 St Matthew
26 St Mary-le-Bow
27 All-Hallows, Bread Street
28 St Mildred, Bread Street
29 St Michael Queenhithe
30 St James Garlickhithe

31 St Michael Paternoster Royal
32 St Mary Aldermary
33 St Antholin
34 St Olave, Old Jewry
35 St Lawrence Jewry
36 St Stephen, Coleman Street
37 St Margaret Lothbury
38 St Mildred Poultry
39 St Stephen Walbrook
40 St Swithun London Stone
41 All-Hallows the Great
42 St Michael, Crooked Lane
43 St Martin Orgar *(rebuilt)*

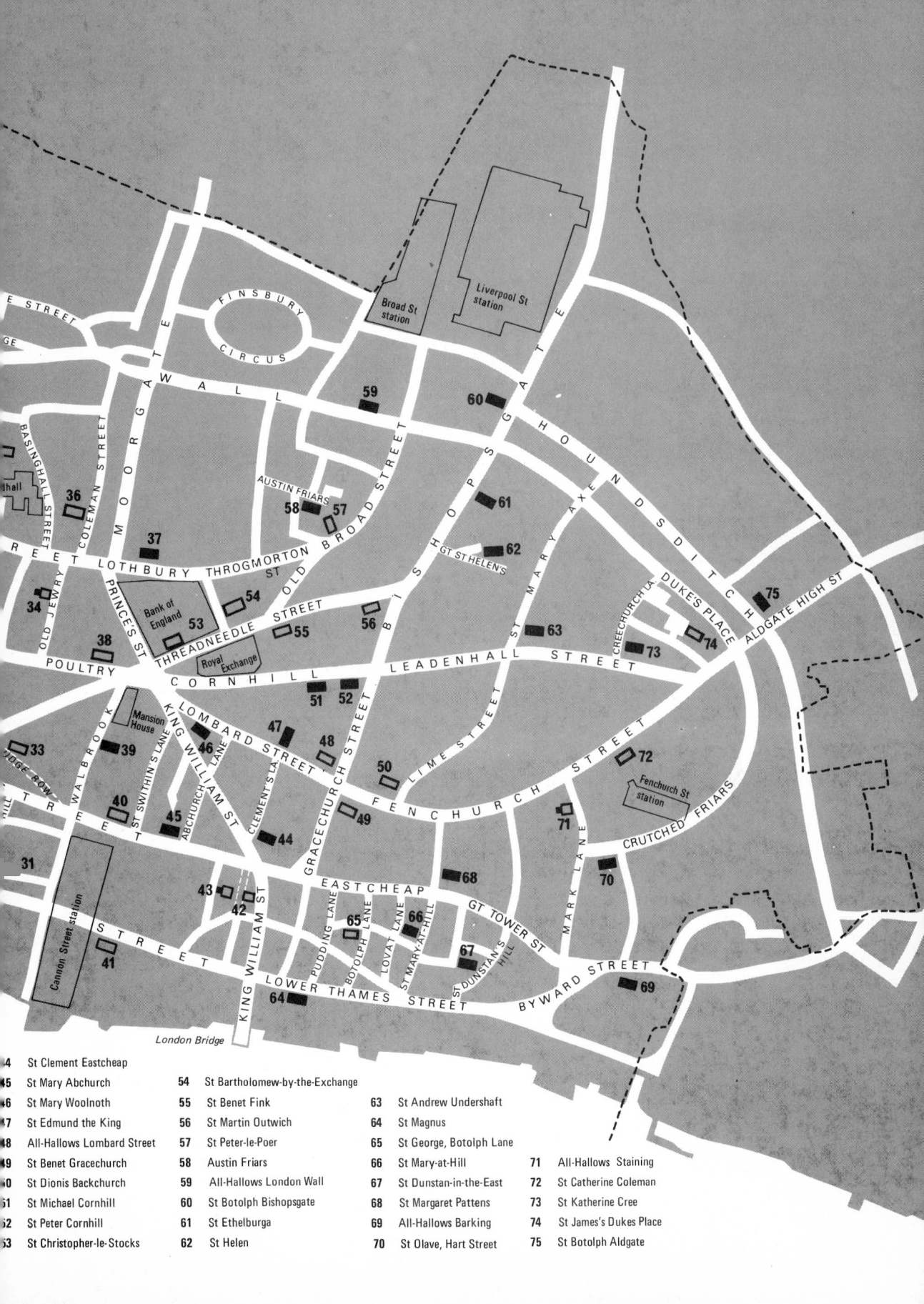

44 St Clement Eastcheap

45 St Mary Abchurch   54 St Bartholomew-by-the-Exchange

46 St Mary Woolnoth   55 St Benet Fink

47 St Edmund the King   56 St Martin Outwich   63 St Andrew Undershaft

48 All-Hallows Lombard Street 57 St Peter-le-Poer   64 St Magnus

49 St Benet Gracechurch   58 Austin Friars   65 St George, Botolph Lane

50 St Dionis Backchurch   59 All-Hallows London Wall   66 St Mary-at-Hill   71 All-Hallows Staining

51 St Michael Cornhill   60 St Botolph Bishopsgate   67 St Dunstan-in-the-East   72 St Catherine Coleman

52 St Peter Cornhill   61 St Ethelburga   68 St Margaret Pattens   73 St Katherine Cree

53 St Christopher-le-Stocks   62 St Helen   69 All-Hallows Barking   74 St James's Dukes Place

                                                             70 St Olave, Hart Street   75 St Botolph Aldgate

Acknowledgements

The Author and Publishers would like to thank the following for permission to reproduce the photographs in this book: All Souls' College, Oxford, nos 15, 16; The Ashmolean Museum, Oxford, nos 2, 3; Country Life, nos 68, 120; John A. Goodall, F.S.A., no. 28; Greater London Council, nos 9, 46, 92, 101, 121, 122, 127, 128, 138, 147; A.F. Kersting, F.R.P.S, nos 29, 49, 57, 116, 137, 141, 145, 148; the National Monuments Record, nos 1, 4, 6–8, 10, 12–14, 17–19, 22–27, 30, 32–45, 47, 48, 50, 51, 53, 54, 59–65, 69, 71–86, 88–91, 93–96, 98, 99, 102–114, 117–119, 123–126, 129–135, 139, 140, 142–144, 149, 150; Sydney W. Newbery, no. 11, 136; Thomas Photos, Oxford, no. 66. The remainder are from the collections of either the Author or the Publisher.

Preface

This book is really a fourth edition of one first published over 30 years ago – during the last war. But so much has happened since 1948, the date of the last edition of *The Old Churches of London*, that this is in some ways a new book.

Unlike its predecessors, I have restricted this edition with a few exceptions to the City Churches, not only because they are so numerous, and include all but three of those designed by Sir Christopher Wren – a very potent reason in itself – but also because they have always been town churches, forming a remarkable series quite distinct from those of now engulfed surrounding villages, or those built in the seventeenth, eighteenth and nineteenth centuries to serve the ever-increasing suburbs.

Also I have been enabled to include as an appendix the latest edition of *London City Churches*, a brief guide to each church – this through the great kindness of the publishers, the Corporation of the City of London. This brings my present book more up to date since all those churches, ruined or damaged in the war, or through subsequent neglect, have now been restored or in a few cases demolished. I would add that this Corporation booklet is on sale as a separate guide at Guildhall or the City Information Centre, St Paul's Churchyard, London EC4, price 25p.

My thanks are due to my friend Robert Harrison, F.S.A., for much valuable information, derived from study of Parish Books, Contracts, etc., at Guildhall and St Paul's Cathedral Library, including dates of many of the Steeples – the last features to be erected – unpublished until the 2nd (1962) edition of the above Guide (see Bibliography). Also for his great kindness in writing out the text of the present book from my nearly unreadable corrections and additions to the last edition.

Also I am indebted to my friend Nicholas Redman, for valuable information and advice.

It only remains for me to express the hope and prayer that this book may help us to value the City churches – precious witnesses to the Things of the Spirit – more than we have done in the past, and to make use of them and back up the work of the Church, so that this remarkable series of buildings may more than justify its existence and be indeed a blessing to all, as their founders intended, to the glory of God.

GERALD COBB
Streatham, 1975

PART I

ONE

The Pre-Fire Churches

In mediaeval times, London was a compact city, mostly confined within its walls and surrounded by small villages, like Shoreditch, Islington or Kensington, now swallowed up in our great Metropolis; while Westminster was a separate community connected with the capital by a great highway through the village of Charing along the 'Strand' of the Thames and down Fleet Street.

At that time, this famous City of London – roughly only one and a half miles long by three-quarters of a mile wide – was thickly populated as now, but by people who not only worked there but lived over their shops or businesses and on Sundays worshipped in their mostly small but astonishingly numerous parish churches.

At the time of the Great Fire of 1666 there were 97 churches within the walls and ten in the 'liberties' which together make up the present 'City'. This number had varied little since at least the thirteenth century, before which, according to Fitz Stephen, there were even more. In his famous description of London, 1186, he says 'There are in London and in the Suburbs 13 churches belonging to convents, besides 126 lesser parish churches'.

This extensive division into many tiny parishes was a peculiar feature of English cities, hardly to be matched elsewhere, and other examples of numerous city churches occurred at Norwich – nearly 60, now only 31; at York – 41, now only 21; Lincoln – 49, drastically reduced in 1549 to 13, and

Winchester – well over 50 (some say 70), now less than a dozen. These reductions in numbers largely coincided with the Reformation, but in London practically all the churches survived that upheaval and continued with one exception until 1666.

Although 'first mention' is seldom before the twelfth century and this no doubt because of the scarcity of early documents, most of the pre-Fire churches, in origin, may well have dated from Saxon times – in London, about a score of them almost certainly did so. How often modern research and excavation reveal origins or foundations of far greater antiquity than previously supposed!

In all these cases, with so many parishes in such small areas (in London some of them were less in size than St Paul's Cathedral) the more popular dedications were repeated many times, and to distinguish churches of the same dedication arose the necessity for the various suffixes that are so delightful a feature of these buildings. They are also found attached to a few solitary dedications – perhaps indicative of early-vanished churches of the same dedication?

In London, St Andrew-by-the-Wardrobe, St Andrew Hubbard, St Andrew Undershaft, St Benet Fink, St Benet Sherehog, St Christopher-le-Stocks, St Dionis Backchurch, St Katherine Cree, St Margaret Moses, St Margaret Pattens, St Martin Orgar, St Martin Outwich, St Martin Pomary, St Martin Vintry, St Mary Abchurch, St Mary Alder-

2 & 3   The City of London east of St Paul's *c.*1550, from a drawing by Anthony Wyngaarde in the Bodleian Library.

mary, St Mary Bothaw, St Mary Mounthaw, St Mary Woolchurch Haw, St Mary Woolnoth, St Michael Bassishaw, St Michael-le-Querne, St Michael Paternoster Royal, St Nicholas Acons, St Nicholas Cole Abbey and St Peter-le-Poer were some of the more curious in the City, while St Clement Danes, St Mary Abbots, St Mary le Bone, St Mary Matfellon (Whitechapel parish church) practically exhaust the parochial examples outside that area.[1]

Before considering the suffixes, to give an idea of the relative popularity of the patron saints, a list of dedications in the City about 1500 is appended, grouped according to the number of examples (see Bond's *Dedications of English Churches*).

One Dedication Only
Holy Sepulchre, usually known as St Sepulchre

St Gabriel the Archangel
St Anne the mother of the Virgin (with St Agnes)[2]
St James the Great,[3] apostle
St John Evangelist, apostle
St Matthew, apostle
St Thomas, apostle
St Dionis (Dionysius the Areopagite, St Paul's convert – the same as St Denis of France)
St Clement,[4] bishop of Rome and possibly St Paul's friend
St Anthony, the famous hermit

---

[1] St Mary of Bethlehem, St Mary Overie, St Mary Rouncevall, St Mary Spittal and Our Lady of the Pew were not parochial.
[2] St Anne Blackfriars was not founded till after the Dissolution.
[3] Garlickhithe (St James's, Duke's Place, existing as Holy Trinity in 1572, was not called St James's till its rebuilding in 1623).
[4] Eastcheap (St Clement Danes is just outside the City).

St Christopher (the Christ-bearer, recalling the famous legend)

St George of Cappadocia, patron of England

St Pancras, a boy martyr

St Agnes, a girl martyr (with St Anne)

St Faith

St Alban, England's first martyr

} Victims of the Diocletian Persecution

St Helen, daughter of 'Old King Cole' and mother of the Emperor Constantine

St Augustine of Hippo, author of the famous *Confessions* (St Augustine Papey)

St Ursula and her 11,000 virgins[1] (with St Mary – St Mary Axe)

St Vedast, bishop of Arras 5th–6th centuries[2]

St Giles, a French hermit 6th or 8th century

St Ewin, Owen, or Audoen. Seems to be the same as St Ouen, who was archbishop of Rouen in 680. There is an ancient church of St Audoen in Dublin

St Bride, i.e. Bridget, a 6th-century Irish saint

St Gregory – Pope Gregory the Great

St Augustine, his apostle to England. (St Augustine, Watling Street, according to Newcourt)

St Ethelburga, abbess of Barking d. *c.*670

St Osyth, nun and martyr, *c.*653 (with St Benet Sherehog)

St Werburgh, a Saxon princess *c.*825 (with St John Evangelist)

St Swithun, bishop of Winchester, 9th century

St Edmund, king of East Anglia, martyred 870

St Alphege, archbishop of Canterbury, martyred 1012

St Magnus, but not the earl of Orkney, martyred 1107, for the church is mentioned in 1067

St Anne and St Agnes, the only double dedication now remaining

NOTE: There appear to have been several other examples of multiple dedications. In the early lists of churches it will be found that in several cases a church seems to change its name from time to time. For example, one that used to stand in the middle of Fenchurch Street is known first as All Hallows Fenchurch (up to about 1320), then for the next 200 years as St Mary Fenchurch (or just Fenchurch), and then St Gabriel or St Mary and St Gabriel Fenchurch. Also, once again – in 1540 – as All-Hallows. A triple dedication?

St Mary the Virgin, St Ursula and the 11,000 virgins, known usually as St Mary Pellipar (*q.v.* p. 19) or St Mary Axe. The latter so named from a relic belonging to the church – one of the three axes said to have been used in executing the virgins

St John Evangelist, known earlier as St Werburgh and in between by both together

St Benet Sherehog and St Osyth.[3] (This latter dedication is commemorated by a fragment of a lane that led up to the site of the church, called Sise Lane)

St Katherine Coleman, which seems to have been known earlier as All Hallows Coleman-church

All Hallows, Barking, which Newcourt says was also dedicated to the Virgin

St Vedast, known in 1352 as St Vedast and St Amandus

Two Dedications

Holy Trinity[4]

St John Baptist

St Bartholomew the apostle[5]

St Mary Magdalen

St Stephen, the first martyr

St Lawrence, said to have been martyred on a gridiron at Rome in 261

St Catherine of Alexandria, tortured on a spiked wheel under Diocletian

St Leonard, 6th-century hermit, patron of prisoners

---

[1] A rare dedication in England. The story of their wanderings and martyrdom at Cologne is wonderfully pictured by Memling on the famous shrine of St Ursula in St John's Hospital at Bruges. See Baring-Gould in his *Curious Myths of the Middle Ages*.

[2] A very rare dedication, the church at Tathwell, Lincs, being the only other in England, though there was formerly one at Norwich.

[3] Or St Sith as Stow has it. Kingsford says (Stow, Add. Notes, p. 16) that this name probably stands for St Zita of Lucca and not for St Osyth as commonly supposed, and he gives early forms: St Cite, Cides or Citha (*temp.* Edward III).

[4] The Priory of Holy Trinity at Aldgate, part of which was also parochial, and Holy Trinity-the-Less (Holy Trinity Minories, just outside the City, as a parish church was not founded till after the Reformation).

[5] St Bartholomew-the-Great and St Bartholomew-by-the-Exchange, then called the Less. The church of the hospital (now St Bartholomew-the-Less) was not made parochial till after the Dissolution.

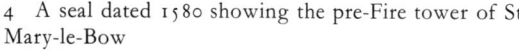

4   A seal dated 1580 showing the pre-Fire tower of St Mary-le-Bow

5   Old All Hallows-on-the-Wall from West and Toms' engraving, 1736.

St Mildred, a Saxon princess, abbess of Minster, Thanet
St Dunstan, archbishop of Canterbury

Three Dedications
St Olave (Olaf), king of Norway, slain 1030

Four Dedications
St Andrew, apostle
St Peter, apostle
St Margaret of Antioch, a shadowy personage
St Nicholas of Myra, patron of children (Santa Claus)
St Benet (Benedict), founder of the famous Order of monks
St Botolph, a 7th-century East Anglian saint

Five Dedications
St Martin, bishop of Tours, who in the 4th century did much to evangelise western France

Seven Dedications
St Michael[1] the archangel

Eight Dedications
All Hallows (All Saints)

Thirteen Dedications
St Mary the Virgin

---

[1] In the thirteenth century there was an eighth, at Aldgate.

Now as to the suffixes. The question 'What do they mean?' is not always easy to answer but it will help if it is remembered that they nearly all fall into one of two categories, derived either from situation or from the name of the founder, benefactor or patron. The rest, about a dozen or so, fall into various classes or are indeterminate.

The following lists are put forward tentatively, for many of these derivations are only guesswork and are open to correction upon fuller knowledge, fresh discoveries or comparison of ancient documents.[1]

Suffixes Derived From Situation
Passing over those with an actual street name,[2] we have:

St Andrew-by-the-Wardrobe, i.e. the King's Wardrobe at Blackfriars established *temp.* Edward III, a branch of the Exchequer for the personal expenditure of the Sovereign

St Christopher-le-Stocks, from the Stocks Market opposite, said to be so named from the instrument of punishment set up there

St James Garlickhithe, from the wharf of that name (hythe, 'a little port or haven to load or unload wares at' – *New World of Words or Universal English Dictionary*, 1720)

St Katherine Cree, properly Creechurch, from the priory of the Holy Trinity or Christ Church[3] in the precincts of which it stood

St Lawrence Jewry, i.e. the Old Jewry – before 1290 when the Jews were expelled from England

St Martin Vintry. The Vintry was the wine merchants' quarter

St Michael Bassishaw, meaning Basing's Hall

St Michael Paternoster Royal or in the Royal, which was a street named after a great tenement called Le Réole or Tower Royal,[4] itself named after the town of Le Réole in Gascony, merchants from which are said to have settled in the neighbourhood. The first part of the suffix, Harben suggests, alludes to Paternoster or rosary makers dwelling near. It was sometimes called Paternoster church.

St Michael Queenhithe, from the wharf, as at St James Garlickhithe

St Nicholas Shambles, from the Shambles, Newgate Street

St Peter Cheap, from Westcheap, i.e. Cheapside

St Swithun London Stone, from the famous stone, supposed by Camden to be a Roman milestone, long set in its wall and still on the site

All Hallows-on-the-Wall, i.e. the City wall

St Andrew Undershaft, known earlier as St Andrew-by-Aldgate, St Andrew Cornhill and 'in 1361 it is called St Andrew Ateknappe (atte Knappe) or "on the hill" from *knap*, O.E. *cnaep*, the top of a hill. St Andrew "atte Shafte" occurs in 1477'.[5] From then onwards called Undershaft, so called says Stow because the famous maypole, set up each year by the door, overtopped the church. But Harben (p. 24) quoting the '*Knape* or Vndershaft' mentioned by Stow, suggests that this was a raised socket for the maypole which, being permanently there, would more likely give name to the church than the pole itself.

St Benet Gracechurch (grass church) from the herb market there

St Mary Pellipar (*pelliparius*, probably bad Latin for *pellarius*, a skinner) from the skinners there dwelling (Stow). Also called St Mary Axe

St Mary Woolchurch Haw, from the beam used for weighing wool in the churchyard, or haw (Stow). It has been suggested (Kingsford II, p. 317) that its name is connected with St Mary Woolnoth to which it was probably a daughter church

St Michael-le-Querne or at the Corn, from the corn market there, *querne* being M.E. hand-mill for crushing corn (Harben)

St Nicholas Cole Abbey, properly Cold Abbey, which seems to have been another name for Cold Harbour which means a shelter for travellers, a 'cold shelter'. As a place name it occurs many times in various parts of the country. In London, besides the famous 'capital messuage'

---

[1] Harben's *Dictionary of London*, 1918 has been invaluable.
[2] Though some of these, like Aldermanbury or Lothbury, are not easy to recognize as such.
[3] It is not clear why a church dedicated to the Holy Trinity should also be called Christ Church but this appears at one time to have been a somewhat frequent practice – Christ Church at Canterbury, near Bournemouth, and at Dublin also being known as Holy Trinity in early documents (Harben, 592).
[4] A street of this name still exists nearby.   [5] Kingsford.

in Thames Street, it is found in the Tower, in Camberwell and Clerkenwell. Also there appears to have been a Cold Abbey in St Sepulchre's parish in 1361. Was there a cold harbour adjacent? The church could hardly be named from the great house as they stood about 600 yards apart and the suffix seems to be earlier than 'first mention' of the house

St Clement Danes, from a settlement of converted Danes (?). This seems the most probable of a number of theories put forward from time to time (Allen's *London*, Vol IV, p. 338)

St Mary-le-Bone (Marylebone parish church), i.e. St Mary at the bourne (the Tybourne)

St Dionis Backchurch, stood back from the road with a row of small houses in front. But Rev. A.R. Winnett points out in his *History of St Dionis Backchurch and St Dionis Parson's Green*, 1935, p. 9, there is mention in a Cotton M.S. of London possessions of Christchurch, Canterbury, of 'The church which Godwin, a clerk surnamed Bac, gave'[1] and he concludes that this was St Dionis which was called 'Bac's church' after him. If this is so, it is a curious coincidence

St Martin Pomary, from an adjacent orchard, *pomarium* (Stow), or from *pomerium*, M. Latin for an open space (?) (Harben, p. 386)

St Mary Bothaw, Stow derives from boat-haw, a boat builder's yard

Suffixes Derived from Name of Founder, Benefactor or Patron

All Hallows, Barking, first mentioned as Berkin-church, 1148, seems originally to have belonged to Barking Abbey which dated from Saxon times.[2]

St Andrew Hubbard

St Benet Fink, from the Finke family of Finke Lane, now Finch Lane, nearby. Stow says Robert Fink the elder rebuilt the church. This bore the suffix 'Finck' as early as 1216–17 (Kingsford II, p. 301)

St Benet Sherehog, 'called St Benet Sorhog before 1248. A wether is called a sherehog when it has once been shorn. The name as applied to the church may be due to some person like Wm. Serehog or Alwyn Serehog who appear in early twelfth-century deeds' (Kingsford II, p. 330).

Also called St Sith. See p. 17, note 3

St Katherine Coleman (?)

St Laurence Pountney, from Sir John Poultney, who made it collegiate

St Margaret Moses or Moyses. A 'Moyses sacerdos', or Moses the priest, occurs in deeds at St Paul's of about 1142

St Margaret Pattens, early form Patyns, from (Stow suggests) patten-makers living near, but derivation from a benefactor seems more probable

St Martin Orgar, from Orgar the deacon who granted the church to St Paul's in the twelfth century

St Martin Outwich, from the Oteswich family: first mention 1216–17

St Mary Abchurch, probably from a man named Abe, Abbe or Abbo (Harben). Not 'Up Church' as Stow

St Mary Colechurch (?)

St Mary Mounthaw, from the family of Mounthaut or Monte Alto

St Mary Woolnoth, from Wulfnoth, probably its founder (Kingsford II, p. 309 and Harben, p. 401)

St Nicholas Acons or Hacon. Hacun was a not-uncommon London name in the twelfth and thirteenth centuries (Kingsford)

St Nicholas Olave

St John Zachary, from a certain Zacharie to whom St John Baptist church was granted by St Paul's canons in the twelfth century, acc. Harben. (It is curious that John Baptist was son of Zacharias.)

Outside the City

St Mary Abbots, Kensington, from the abbey of Abingdon to whom it was given in 1111

Comparative Suffixes

All Hallows-the-Great and All Hallows-the-Less

St Bartholomew-the-Great and St Bartholomew-the-Less

St Dunstan-in-the-East and St Dunstan-in-the-West

---

[1] Kingsford confirms this under heading of St Dionis (Add. Notes, p. 10).

[2] A Saxon doorway was discovered at All Hallows in 1941 (see p. 141).

6 Old St Dunstan-in-the-West before removal of the little shops along the south side; from West and Toms' engraving, 1739

7 St Bartholomew-the-Great, showing pre-Fire reredos – painted on canvas. Original drawing for Wilkinson's *Londina Illustrata*

Suffixes of Various Meanings

St Mary Aldermary, meaning that this is, Elder Mary, the oldest founded St Mary's in the City (?)

St Mary-le-Bow, or de Arcubus, supposed to refer to the arches of the eleventh-century crypt, which probably also gave its name to the Court of Arches held in this church or vestry.[1] (There is a St Mary-le-Bow at Durham, a St Mary Arches at Exeter, and until lately a St Peter at Arches in Lincoln)

[1] It cannot refer to the flying buttresses of the old steeple, for the suffix was in use three or four centuries before that was built.

8   North side of the choir, St Bartholomew-the-Great

9   South-west corner of St Bartholomew-the-Less, 1906

It is curious that these two churches are at opposite ends of the same lane.

St Augustine Papey. It has been suggested (Kingsford's *Stow*, II, p. 293) that as this church belonged to Holy Trinity Priory of Augustinian Canons at Aldgate, and as the relics of St Augustine were preserved in an Augustinian church at Pavia (Papia), it may have been named after that town. Also in the register of Aldgate Priory it is referred to as St Augustine *pavie juxta murum* (Harben). But there is still the question 'Why?' Also, anchorites appear to have been known among the northmen as 'Papas'. Did one so called live near this church? (Harben)

All Hallows Staining, Mark Lane, early mentioned, 1170–87, as 'Stanenchirche in Cradockes lane', a turning out of Mark Lane. Stow calls it 'All Hallows Stane Church'. The name is explained by reference to *parochia de Stanenetha* (stonehithe) at London in 1194. '"Stonwarf" in All Hallows Barking [parish] occurs in 1304' (Kingsford II, p. 308)

St Mary Staining, near Wood Street, early mentioned as *Ecclesia de Staningehage*, 1189. Professor Maitland suggests 'Staningehage' means the haws (yards) of the men of Staines in London. 'The Confessor had granted to St Peter, Westminster, the manor of Staines, with the land called Staeningehage within London . . .' (Kingsford II, p. 340). Later references are 'Church of Stainingelane', 1275, 'St Mary de Stanigeslane', 1278, and 'St Mary Stanynges', c.1460.

St Mary Somerset. Kingsford found mention of it in a deed of 1170–87 and suggests the suffix may be derived from Ralph de Sumery who occurs about the same time. Other early references are St Marie de $\overline{Sum}$ $\overline{sat}$ (*temp.* Richard I), St Mary de Sumersate and St Mary de Somersete, c.1272

St Peter-le-Poer or le Poor was so called because 'sometime, peradventure, a poore Parish' (Stow). Until the sixteenth century was known as 'St Peter Bradstrete'.

Outside the City

St Mary Matfellon had early forms Mantefelune, 1280, and Mattefelon or Matrefelun, 1282. Povah (Annals of St Olave, Hart Street) says that Matfellon meant a fuller's teazle and referred to the fullers in the neighbourhood, but actually it is Old French for the centaury or knapweed, and as surnames similar to it occur in the fourteenth century (and a John de Knopwed, mercer, died in 1341) Kingsford thinks the suffix perpetuates a benefactor

St Mary Overy. Stow 'St Mary over the Rie or Overie, that is, over the water', but the true derivation of Overy seems to be from 'Oferes', O.E. for 'at the bank'. Thus the name means St Mary of Bankside (Kingsford, Add. Notes, p. 27, and Canon Thompson's *St Saviour's, Southwark*) The church was made parochial and renamed St Saviour by Henry VIII; it is now Southwark Cathedral.

It is curious that in two cases in this class a church is or was situated in a street bearing a name that is a corruption of that of the church:

St Vedast, Foster Lane, where Foster is evolved from Vedast by such steps as Vastes, Fastes,

Fastres, Faster, Faister and Fauster, as shown by W. Sparrow Simpson in his *Life and Legend of St Vedast*[1]

St Olave, Tooley Street, Southwark, where Tooley is corrupted from St Olave, evidently by similar transition. According to Baynes' *History of Norwich*, p. 132, there was formerly a St Olave's, Tooley Street, in that city also, and St Tooley's is given as an alternative name for the church.

NOTE: The following list referring to All Hallows-the-Great will demonstrate how the suffixes varied from time to time.[2] A.H. le Grant, 1259; A.H. at the Hay, 1271–2; All Saints over Hey Wharf; A.H. the Great in the Corderie, 1318; A.H. next the street of the Corders, 1326; A.H. the Great in the Ropery, 1332; A.H. called le Mechele, 1379; A.H. the More in Thames St, 1537. It also seems to be identical with 'A.H. Semanes-cherche', twelfth to thirteenth centuries.[3]

All these curious names date from mediaeval times, occurring again and again in wills, inventories and other documents, some few from before the Conquest. In this connection it is noteworthy that one church has earned notoriety and privileges through a tradition that exaggerated its antiquity. St Peter, Cornhill, still possesses a framed inscription on brass said to date from before 1666, setting forth its claim to have been founded by a certain King Lucius in A.D. 179, and on the strength of this assertion the rector claimed precedence over all the other City parsons, which formerly involved the privilege of coming last among them 'as their Abbot or Prior' in the Whitsuntide processions. This was confirmed to him in 1417, these rights having been disputed by the rectors of St Magnus and St Nicholas Cole Abbey in favour of themselves. But it does not appear why these two rectors were so important.[4]

The emoluments of one church, St Augustine Papey, became so small that no priest could be

---

[1] This church for 100 years and more before the Great Fire was almost always known as St Foster's, and until recent times as St Vedast, alias Foster.

[2] Harben's *Dictionary of London*, p. 15.

[3] Ibid. pp. 17–18.

[4] Also when the Union of Benefices Act was passed in 1860, St Peter's was expressly exempted from its working.

induced to accept the cure, so the parish was united to that of its neighbour, All Hallows-on-the-Wall, which was also very poor. This was about 1430, and in 1442 the disused church was appropriated as the chapel of an almshouse, then founded, for superannuated City clergy, the admirable rules for which are still preserved.

On the other hand, some churches were very prosperous, and in three cases a parish church was made also collegiate (that is, instead of the rector only, a college of priests was established to serve it); it is noteworthy that they were all near neighbours in lanes north of Thames Street, and all the colleges were founded by famous men:

At St Lawrence, Candlewick Street, by Sir John Poultney, 1332–47.

At St Michael, Crooked Lane by Sir William Walworth, 1381.

At St Michael Royal, by Sir Richard Whittington, 1410.

In the case of St Michael, Crooked Lane, this led to the church being enlarged with chapels, etc., making it cruciform on plan. It also had a s.w. chapel appropriated to the Fishmongers' Company. And it appears to have had a (charnel?) chapel in the churchyard.

Sometimes there were parochial chapels apart from the parish church, as the Chapel of the Blessed Mary of Conyhope Lane in the parish of St Mildred Poultry, afterwards used by a Guild of Corpus Christi. Also, in the burial ground of All Hallows, Barking, was a famous chapel founded by Richard I, and said to have been made collegiate for a dean and six canons by Richard III (Stow).

A number of churches had cloisters – a very unusual appendage for a parish church. But of this, more later on.[1]

As regards the situations of the churches, many of them were extremely close together, as St Peter and St Michael, Cornhill, which have less than their own length between them, while St Olave Jewry and St Martin Pomary were almost touching, and must have shared the same churchyard! And several of them had curious positions. All Hallows-the-Less was partly over a gateway – that leading to 'the capital messuage called Cold harbor'[2] (Stow).

St Faith under St Paul's, as its name implied, was in the crypt of the cathedral; to which the parishioners were relegated when an extension of St Paul's in the thirteenth century necessitated the demolition of their church. St Gregory-by-St Paul's was attached to the west front of the cathedral on the south side. The position of these two churches led Fuller (*Worthies of England*) to write of St Paul's that it was 'a Mother's Church indeed, having one babe in her body, St Faith's, and another in her arms, St Gregory's'.

St Gabriel Fenchurch stood in the middle of the road like the Strand churches of today. All Hallows-on-the-Wall and the first St Alphege were built against the City wall, while of the four St Botolph's, three were situated just outside a City gate, while the fourth was near Billingsgate, which was probably a Roman water gate. St Botolph was regarded as the patron of travellers.

Occasionally a church changed its position, as St Stephen Walbrook, which originally stood on the west side of the stream, but in 1429 it moved its situation to the east bank, and after the laying of numerous foundation stones, a fine church was erected (much larger than its successor, Wren's masterpiece) on land given by Robert Chicheley, whose brother, Henry Chicheley, was rector of the old church in 1396, afterwards archbishop of Canterbury and founder of All Souls' College, Oxford. Another church that changed its site was St Alphege, London Wall, which, at the dissolution of the monasteries, abandoned its old quarters on the wall for the fourteenth-century chapel of Elsing Priory opposite, which became the parish church and of which the crossing still remains.

With so many churches so close together it would have been surprising if they had been either large or very beautiful, and judging from examples that have come down to us or of which we have records, it seems that 'the mediaeval parish churches of London were in no wise remarkable architecturally'. The small churches of St Ethelburga and St Olave, Hart Street are typical of the vast majority of the

---

[1] In the chapter on Churchyards.
[2] In Bristol the tower and spire of St John's Church are over a city gate, and other examples of building churches or chapels over gates exist at Winchester, Warwick and formerly at Canterbury.

10　The south porch of St Sepulchre, looking out

11　St Olave, Hart Street: glimpse of vestry (1662) through earlier south-east door of church

City churches before the Great Fire.[1] Another fact that emerges is rather curious – none of them appears to have had a structural chancel, though outside the City, Old St Giles and St Martin-in-the-Fields had this feature (in the latter case only added in 1609), and there may have been other examples.

From what we can glean, it seems that All Hallows, Barking, St Dunstan-in-the-East, St Stephen Walbrook, St Mary Aldermary, St Mary-le-Bow, and, outside the Walls, St Bride, St Sepulchre and St Giles Cripplegate, were among the largest and finest of the mediaeval City churches, the two latter having commanding towers. St Dunstan-in-the-East and St Laurence Pountney had lofty spires, and St Mary-le-Bow was dis-

tinguished by a form of steeple unique in the south of England, though it had counterparts at St Nicholas, Newcastle, St Giles, Edinburgh, and King's College, Aberdeen. The tower had at the corners four stone lanterns, and a fifth was held aloft between them on flying buttresses, forming an open crown that must have been very beautiful.[2] This church, though rebuilt by Wren, retained its

---

[1] Quotation from *The Royal Commission on Historic Monuments, Inventory of the City*, p. 25. It should be remembered that St Bartholomew-the-Great and St Helen owe their distinction to the monastic element.

[2] Stow says that the lanterns were intended to be glazed and lit at night the convenience of travellers. See note 5, p. 153.

eleventh-century crypt until the Second World War. It consisted of a nave and side aisles, the former of which was divided into 12 bays by six pillars supporting a groined vault. Three of these pillars remained, but the vault was renewed in brick by Wren. The north aisle vault was original; the south aisle walled-up and inaccessible. After the war, the whole crypt was opened up and largely renewed.

The way secular buildings were erected against the churches and diminutive shops masked their façades was reminiscent of many foreign towns (both these practices were continued after 1666, the former down to the present day) and necessitated by the excessively high land values in the City. This practice was once common in this country, as it is still on the Continent, but these in London must be almost the only examples left in England. Of these encroachments the following are some examples. Old St Dunstan-in-the-West and Wren's St Margaret, Lothbury had little shops cluttering up their frontages, and St Ethelburga and St Dionis Backchurch had tiny houses with shops beneath. These two latter lasted till modern times, and St Stephen Walbrook until 1941 had one such house against the tower, while at St Bartholomew-the-Great, the verger's red-brick dwelling still sits comfortably on the north aisle. Unfortunately it appears to be regarded as an eyesore, for photographers seem always to avoid it. St Mildred, Bread Street, was so surrounded by modern offices that only the façade could be seen and until shortly before the Second World War the same could be said of St Edmund, while a few yards away from the latter, All Hallows, Lombard Street, was so hemmed in by banks, etc., that it was known as 'the Church Invisible'. It had a narrow yard at each side and access to it was only to be had by passages under the surrounding houses. Until 1941, the only churches in the City entirely detached from other buildings were St Andrew-by-the-Wardrobe, St Benet, Paul's Wharf, St Lawrence Jewry, St Bartholomew-the-Less, St Bride, the three St Botolphs, and except for a small watch-house, blitzed but now rebuilt, St Sepulchre: i.e. three inside and six outside the walls.

To conclude this chapter, below are some extracts

from Vestry Minutes and Churchwardens Accounts both before and after the Great Fire.

GIFTS TO DISTRESSED AREAS AND PERSONS

In 1645 the parishioners of St Alban and St Michael, Wood Street sent contributions from collections made at preachings to 'the maimed and wounded Soldiers', 'their widows', the 'distressed Irish', as well as to districts round Bristol and Manchester. Also for the relief of Taunton, held by Colonel Massey for Parliament, they sent £20 3s. 10d. Also 'musquetts and old clothes'.

At St Swithun:

1642 To Mr Underwood for ye poor
      maymed solders   £2. 3. 4.
1652 To the poor of Barkin towards theyre
      loss by fire   £6. 3. 2.

After this munificence the following is rather an anticlimax:

1695 To the people of Essex their land
      being drowned   2. 6.

PAROCHIAL 'CHARITY'

The parochial dealings with the poor and wretched were niggardly in the extreme. Entries of money given to beggars and women with child, to hurry them out of the parish and so save the rates, occur again and again. Even in the plague years, sufferers in the streets were treated in the same way.

St Swithun:

1661 For getting several people out of the
      Parish   8.
1679 Pd for clearing the Parish of a woman
      bigg with childe   1. 0.
1702 To coach hire to carry a poor woman
      to prevent her dying in ye parish   2. 0.

PARISH FOUNDLINGS

1690 Laid out for Jasper Swithen for Cloath Coat
      and Breeches, Bed, bolster and Blanket, Hat and
      Hatband, Shoes and Stockings as per Receipt
      and 12d. expence at the same time   £1. 16. 0.

(See also p. 29, St Stephen Walbrook, 1640–41.)

Later are the following curious entries:

DRINKS FOR WOMEN AND CHILDREN

1715 Pd for Canary to give the women and
      children in church on Ascension Day   1. 0.

12   Old St Martin Outwich (rebuilt 1798, demolished 1874)

1717 To Mr Read for seven bottles of Sack
   in the vestry for the children   14. 0.

DINNERS ON HOLY THURSDAY (ASCENSION DAY)
This was a great day for every Parish, when the bounds were beaten and 'perambulation dinners' were occasions for great expense. The religious significance of the day seems to have been largely neglected.
St Swithun again:
1675 Pd for poynts and ribbons on Holie
   Thursdaye and for a dinner   £8. 19. 2

Whether 'poynts' were tagged laces, as one would ordinarily assume, or pointed wands for beating the bounds is not clear, as 'ribbons' are mentioned as well.
Easter 1690 Pd upon the Accountt of the
   Parish Dinner on Holy Thursday for a
   Surloyne of beef. Bringing home, weigh-
   ing 4 pound and 5 stone without suet   11. 0
Pd for a basket of Asperagus (3s.) and for a
   pound of tobacco (5s.)   8. 0
Pd at the Poops Head for Wine and other
   things   £6. 4. 0

13   Pre-Fire pulpit, St Helen, Bishopsgate

14 Pre-Fire pulpit, All Hallows-by-the-Tower. The door and ironwork survive

Pd the poulterer for ffowels (38s.) and pd
  Mr Bentley, Cook (31s.)   £3. 9. 0
Pd for Westphaly Hams   £1. 8. 0

Visible reminders of these occasions were to be seen everywhere in the City (mostly on the walls at first-floor level) and a number still remain – the little parish boundary marks, usually in the form of metal tablets with the initials of the church and a date in relief, many of them of charming design. They were erected and maintained to define the exact extent of each parish and annually checked on Ascension Day by Beating the Bounds.

SEPARATION OF THE SEXES IN CHURCH

At St Mary Colechurch the custom prevailed of separating the sexes in church, and lists occur ranging in date from 1613–61 giving the names of the pew owners, first the men's side and then the women's. This segregation also obtained at St Magnus.

WHIPPING POSTS

At St Stephen Walbrook it was agreed in Vestry, 15 October 1598, 'That ther should be a poste sete up be ffore our church to punish vagaraunte begares' and in St Mary Woolchurch Accounts:

1601 Paid to Andrews for whipping the
     vagrants for one whole yeare   5. 4
1611 Paid to Robert Andrews for yiorne-
     worke for the whiping post   2. 8

And lastly in St Stephen Walbrook's Accounts are these entries:

1637–38 Pd for Rosemary and Bayes to
        adorne y Church at Christmas   3. 0
1640–41 Pd and spent on the Gossips
        (godparents) at the Christening of
        Stephen Oylbut found in the Barge
        Yard upon an Oyl Butt[1]   3. 6

---

[1] Foundlings were commonly given names (often far from kind) reminiscent of the parish where discovered, as Benetfink (St Benet Fink), Bartholomew Exchange and Bartholomew Threadneedle (St Bartholomew-by-the-Exchange) and Martyne Felde (St Martin-in-the-Fields).

TWO

The Churches of Sir Christopher Wren: The Building and Accounts

The scene from Blackfriars Bridge must have been an unforgettable sight in the eighteenth century before tall warehouses began to hide the sides of St Paul's cathedral, rising majestically over the crowded roofs of the rebuilt City; and, later, before the demolitions among the churches had nearly halved the wonderful array of aspiring beauty which Wren's varied steeples presented to the fascinated spectator. This mass of slender erections, pointing like blunt and sharp pencils to heaven, formed as it were a retinue to St Paul's, stretching from the east up to the cathedral as it looked towards the setting sun, with Christ Church, St Martin's and St Bride's as forerunners. Alas, nowadays the vision is utterly spoiled by wholesale riverside demolitions and the erection of towering blocks of offices – arrogant and incongruous – that now dominate the City.

After the great calamity commemorated by the Monument, the grand period of our subject is in sight. But we should remember that if Wren had had his way, the historic City, with its curving streets and multitude of churches, would have perished for ever. His plan for a model City provided for no more than 19 parish churches, disposed at intervals along the principal streets and other prominent positions. And to accommodate the crowded population, they would have had to be larger and handsomer than any he actually built.

But the impossibility of delaying rebuilding until a complete clearance had been effected prevented any such destruction of the ancient plan (a result threatened by modern development!). With a cathedral and over 80 parish churches in ruins, 51 of which, besides St Paul's, it was at length decided to rebuild, surely there was never a greater opportunity for a great architect, and with Sir Christopher Wren surely there was seldom a man who so rose to an occasion or used an opportunity to such advantage! Superintending the vast works of the cathedral, and having on his hands the erection of royal and palatial buildings at Winchester, Hampton Court, Kensington, Chelsea and Greenwich, and planning a great palace in Whitehall, besides many other works in London, Oxford, Cambridge and elsewhere, it is remarkable that he was able to give to these City shrines such sympathetic care as undoubtedly he did – the churches themselves are witnesses thereto.

Before coming to consider Wren's churches in detail, something must be said as to how they were erected. From various causes it was a slow process. Complicated questions respecting the rights of patrons, impropriators, rectors, etc., had to be settled, as also, most important, which churches should be rebuilt. It was four years before even a start was made, when 16 were begun; while disputes between unwillingly united parishes and the

15   A preliminary study by Wren for St Bride, Fleet Street

impossibility of obtaining sufficient Portland stone and other materials to build them all at once – to say nothing of labour – all contributed to prolong the delay, so that the last six churches to be built were not started till 20 years after their predecessors had been destroyed and most of the steeples were not completed until the eighteenth century.

TEMPORARY ACCOMMODATION

In the meantime the people had to worship somewhere, and various were the expedients adopted to provide the necessary accommodation. Some of the stronger ruins were temporarily roofed over, as at St Michael, Wood Street, where the mediaeval remains were discovered incorporated in Wren's church when it was demolished in 1896. Some of the City companies lent their restored or newly-built halls, as did the Stationers' to the parishioners of St Martin, Ludgate, and the Salters' to those of St Swithun. In addition to which eight meeting houses were taken over for use by the established church.

In 1669, All Hallows-the-Great solved its own problem by erecting in the burial ground a temporary church, or 'Tabernacle' as it was called, and in the following year the idea was taken up by the authorities, and nine more similar buildings were put up; these with All Hallows were afterwards increased to 30. The accounts for these places of worship survive, and show widely varying costs, from £265 for St Mary Abchurch, to only £50 for St Pancras, Soper Lane.[1] In 1672 the parishioners of St Peter, Cornhill, were so pleased with their Tabernacle that they presented Wren with £5 for his pains in erecting it.[2]

FINANCE OF THE REBUILDING

51 churches were at length ordered to be rebuilt, the cost to be borne by the Government, and paid for out of a tax of 1s. on every 'chaldron' or ton of coals coming into London, which proving quite inadequate was later increased to 3s.

'The co-operation of the citizens was required, and each parish had to deposit £500 with the Commissioners for the rebuilding before the work could begin, this money being ultimately repaid. Sometimes as apparently in the case of

St Stephen Walbrook progress made in building overran the funds available and money had to be borrowed at high rates of interest on the security of the coal dues'.[3]

This provision was only for the structural work; the fittings etc., had to be provided by the parishioners themselves and/or special donors, though in a few cases these latter also contributed to the building expenses, and in two cases fittings were paid for by the Commissioners – at St Andrew-by-the-Wardrobe and St Mary Somerset.

UNION OF PARISHES

The parishes of the 35 churches not rebuilt were each united to one whose church was to rise again[4] but each continued to function as a separate parish with vestries and churchwardens as before. In the nineteenth century when churches began to be pulled down as redundant, this system often led to one church having to serve several parishes (in two cases, six and in one case, seven) with the result that some rectors had anything up to a dozen churchwardens to assist them.

WREN'S WORKMEN

The building accounts are preserved in St Paul's cathedral library and in the Rawlinson MSS. in the Bodleian Library, Oxford.[5] These give the names of many of the able workmen and craftsmen who carried out Wren's designs and seem to establish that he found ready to hand hereditary firms of tradesmen. Some members of these, it seems, had worked for Inigo Jones, who died in 1652, only about ten years before Wren started practising as an architect; and it is safe to say that without these capable workmen he could never have accomplished such immense tasks of which rebuilding the City churches was but one.

The accounts in St Paul's are what we may call 'Working Copies' and they extend to c.1717, thus

---
[1] Bell's *Great Fire of London*, p. 306. Also see biblio. p. 181.
[2] Lon. & Middx. Arch. Soc. Trans. Vol. IV, p. 305.
[3] Bell's *Great Fire of London*, 1666, p. 310.   [4] *Ibid.*, p. 311.
[5] See Paper by Sir Lawrence Weaver in *Archaeologia* Vol 66 given on 10 December 1914 and Wren Society Vol x 1933.

16   A preliminary study by Wren for St Edmund, Lombard Street

covering the completion of the various steeples most of which were only finished after 1700. These copies seem to have escaped notice until unearthed by Mr R.H. Harrison, who thus established the dates and costs of these crowning features of Wren's churches.

But the accounts in the Bodleian, as described by Weaver, only extend to 1695. They are evidently 'Fair Copies', being models of neatness and penmanship; and they may well have been written by Nicholas Hawksmoor who was in Wren's office and was paid for copying out three books of accounts.

They comprise three volumes:

    B 387 The Bills of the Parochial Churches

    B 388 Ledger of the Parochial Churches

    B 389 Tabernacle Ledger and General Account

Taking the last first it appears that the tabernacles were constructed of timber on a brick base, the fittings being severely simple, as for example those for St Mary Aldermary:

Joiners Work

Pulpit and type (sounding board)	£5. 0. 0
Communion table	£1. 0. 0
Reading desk and clerk's desk	£2. 10. 0
Total	£8. 10. 0

From the General Account (in the same volume) some interesting facts emerge:

Aug 31, 1671 'To Christopher Wren, his disbursements to Samuel Wells for drawing paper, paper books, pencills parchment etc. as appears by bill, June 1670–May 1671, the Summe of   £7. 16. 6.'

But Wren's average expenditure on drawing paper etc. to 1679 was about £12 a year. And Wren's domestic clerk, Nicholas Hawksmoor, in 1687 got £9 'for finding ink, paper, books, wafers, pens and other necessary for ¾ of a year'.

The Ledger of the Parochial Churches (B388) is of much less interest and shows only the payments of the tradesmen's bills and an abstract of the totals paid to each man.

In B387 the bills themselves are given and several interesting points regarding the work should be noted. Although these accounts deal primarily with constructional work they include a certain amount on decoration, and much ordinary carving

such as capitals, etc. was done by masons and joiners, while bricklayers had no monopoly of bricklaying, much of which was done by masons. Joiners only did 'right wainscot work', that is only the best and most elaborate work, but carpenters often did wainscot doors. In almost every case the roofing was of lead, so that nearly an eighth of the total building costs was paid to plumbers – £31,468. Among the plasterers, there was a sort of partnership between Henry Doogood and John Grove who, either together or separately did most of the churches, and at St Vedast Thompson the mason, Willcox a carpenter, 'partners with Christopher Russell, bricklayer', took an 'agreement by the great' or as we should say a lump sum contract, at £1,250 and paid the plumber, plasterer, glazier and smith.[1]

Also among the craftsmen appear a small number of women's names as 'Sarah Freeman, plumber' (St James Garlickhithe) Widdow Pearce, Painter (St Magnus), Widow Cleer, Joiner (All Hallows, Lombard Street), Ann Brooks, Smith (St Michael Royal) and others. Evidently it was a custom for widows to carry on the businesses of their deceased husbands.

The total cost of rebuilding the 51 City churches according to the Bodleian accounts was £263,786 but this does not include the majority of the steeples which, from the St Paul's accounts would add approximately a further £63,000.

Weaver says, without quoting his authority, that Wren got five per cent on the cost of each church, which would 'put over £13,000 into Wren's pocket, a small enough sum for so superb an amount of work'. On this basis the steeples etc. would have brought in a further £3,150.

The following are a few extracts taken from the Building Accounts. St Mary-le-Bow, being connected with the archbishop of Canterbury's Court of Arches, was always of great importance and, as related in an earlier chapter, possessed a remarkable tower which, it appears, was not badly damaged in the Fire. £640 was spent on its attempted restora-

---

[1] Weaver 'Complete Building Accounts of the City Churches (Parochial) designed by Sir Christopher Wren'. *Archaeologia* Vol 66, p. 7–8. Actually, this is not quite correct as £550 had already been paid for repairs, on account, before the above agreement was made.

tion and that of the church. But when rebuilding was seen to be inevitable, it was decided to emphasize the importance of the church by building a magnificent steeple and bringing it forward to Cheapside (previously it seems it had stood back from the street) with a vestibule between it and the church.

After accounts for repairing and then for demolishing the old tower, there follow those of Thomas Cartwright and John Thompson, Masons, for building the new tower. The following items are included:

ffor ye Pyramid	£80
ffor ye 4 Pinicles with ye carving	£250
ffor 4 Urnes with ye flames	£20
ffor Scaffolding in consideration of ye Greate height	£30
ffor making moddells	£10

Other bills:

To Edward Pearce, Mason, for carving of a wooden Dragon for a moddell for ye Vane of copper upon ye top of ye Steeple and cutting a relive in board to be preferred up to discern the right bigness, the summe of £4

To Robert Bird Coppersmith for work done by him . . . about and in ye Neck Ball & Dragon, September 25 1679 £60. 13. 9
This includes £38 for making the dragon.

To Thos Laine, Painter,
ffor Guilding the Urnes Ball and Dragon £14. 2. 0

The complete charges for the new tower and spire amounted to £7,388. 8. 7½. while that of the church, £8,033. 0. 5 brought the total cost of St Mary-le-Bow to £15,421. 9. 0½ – the most expensive of Wren's City churches. St Bride ran it close with £15,203. 13. 6½ while St Matthew, Friday St, the cheapest of all, cost no more than £2,301. 8. 2.

A good second example is St Stephen Walbrook, built between 1672–1682 except for the steeple. The masons were Thomas Strong and Christopher Kempster. In their carving bill they charge £7 each for the capitals of the 16 Corinthian pillars, £1 less than Cartwright for similar work at St Mary-le-Bow which are only half caps, whereas these at St Stephen are whole ones. Another item:

ffor carving two scrolls at the west Dore £1. 10. 0

In John Longland the Carpenter's account he

charges:

ffor 34 Sqs[1] ¼ 5f. of Roofing in the Dome at £9	£308. 10. 0
ffor the Lanthorne on the top of ye Dome att	£60. 0. 0

Grove and Doogood the Plasterers charge:

ffor 351 yds in ye Dome fretted with mouldings roses and palmes	£150. 0. 0
ffor 24 f. of Cornice in ye Lanthorne 1f. 8in. girt at ii[s]	£2. 8. 0
ffor a foliage flower in ye top of ye Lanthorne 4ft 6in. over	£0. 10. 0
ffor 23 f. of moulding at bottom of ye Lanthorne 20in. deep at xviii[d]	£1. 14. 6
ffor 26 f ½ of foliage twisted round a staff at bottom of ye Lanthorne 10 f 6in. girt [girth?] iis.vid.	£3. 6. 3

Altogether their accounts total £494 12s. 8d.
See Wren Soc. X.

LAYING OF FOUNDATION STONES:
(From Vestry Minutes) Following the example of 1429 there was an elaborate stone-laying ceremony, when the first stones in rebuilding the church were laid in the east foundation by the following persons:

The Lord Mayor, Sir Robert Hanson
Sir Thomas Chitchley (Privy Council), a descendant of the founder of the earlier church.[2]
Sir John Robinson, Lieut. of the Tower
Six officials of the Grocers' Company, the patrons
The rector, Robert Marriott, and four leading parishioners
The two churchwardens (one of whom was Major Adrian Quiney, whose Uncle Thomas was Shakespeare's son-in-law)
(17 December 1672)

DINNER TO WREN AND HIS LADY:
In the Churchwardens Accounts is the following:
7 March 1673 Paid for a dinner at the Swan in Old Fish Street to entertain Dr Wren . . . with the vestry and others £9. 9. 0

EFFORTS TO HASTEN REBUILDING:
'Paid to ye Survaer Gennerall by order of Vestry

---

[1] Square=a square of timber 10 ft × 10 ft.

[2] Sir Thomas sent £100 towards the rebuilding 4 April 1673.

for a gratuety to his Lady to incuridg and hast in ye rebuilding ye church twenty ginnes' in a silk purse. (The gift to Lady Wren is a subtle touch!)

6 May 1673 Spent at several vestries and other occasions in prompting the rebuilding the church this year £8. 3. 0

The completion of the church, in 1679, was celebrated by another dinner, this time at the Bull's Head Tavern, and the rector, Sir Christopher, Longland, Strong, Kempster, Davies, College, Creecher, Davies, painter, and others were invited, and a further £10 was presented to Lady Wren. Sir Christopher and his principal tradesmen are mentioned as being invited to these dinners till 1685. They must have been pleasant occasions. In the Accounts, 1680–81, is this item:

Paid for a hogshead of Claret presented to Sir Chr. Wren £9. 10. 0

It is good to know that the vestry made gifts out of gratitude as well as by way of a bribe!

If the parishioners' wishes had prevailed, the church would have had a prominent feature facing the Stocks Market, for after failing, in 1673, to get the tower brought forward, they petitioned in 1681 for leave to acquire land for 'a handsome and ornamental Porch' but although the market folk declared they would be satisfied with £20 as compensation, nothing came of it although Wren produced a design, and offers were made for 'a handsome clock and dyall', drawings for which remain at Guildhall Library.

As it is now, most of the church is hidden by the Mansion House and the lower part of the tower was masked by the charming little house, originally the clerk's dwelling, latterly rebuilt or altered and until its destruction in the last war, a bookseller's shop and disfigured by hideous posters. Between it and the church was the delightful eighteenth-century 'Gothick' window of the vestry.

PEWING

The parishioners of St Stephen Walbrook showed themselves fastidious regarding their comfort during services, for they sent round (7 February 1676) to several churches – St Nicholas Cole Abbey, St Edmund, St Mary-at-Hill, St Stephen, Coleman Street and St Bride – to report which was 'the best to take patterns by in order to the pewing

the Church' and two years later it was decided to copy St Nicholas. They also directed that the pulpit be something like that of St Lawrence Jewry.[1]

Further extracts relating to this church are given in the chapter on Fittings.

EXTRAS

At St James Garlickhithe (1676–83), when the church was nearly finished, in 1682, these items were paid (among others):

For Church Bible and Common Prayer £3. 3. 0
Two bottles of sherry and pipes at the
 opening of the church 3. 4
Hire of 3 dozen cushions and porterage 13. 4
Wine when the Lord Mayor and Aldermen
 were at our Church £1. 11. 0
Wax Links to enlighten my Lord Mayor
 home 4. 6

In the Vestry Book for 19 July 1682, an entry appears that Mr Thomas Osborn, churchwarden, was to pay Wren's two clerks 40s. each 'for their care and kindness in hastening the building of the church, and to induce them to do the like for the more speedy finishing of the Steeple'

STEEPLES – THE LAST FEATURES FINISHED

In many cases Wren built his steeples in two stages, the first, the tower proper, so designed that it could stand as such if necessary, but if and when more money was forthcoming, a spire or other elaboration could be added. In a panorama of London by Georg Balthasar Probst (between 1707 and 1714) St James Garlickhithe, St Michael Royal and St Stephen Walbrook are all shown as having plain towers with urns at the corners within which the present steeples were afterwards built. At St Magnus, although the church was finished in 1679, the steeple was not completed until 1705, and at St Mildred, Poultry (united with St Mary Colechurch) the parishioners did not give up hopes of a spire for years, as the following entry in the Churchwardens Accounts for 1717–18 shows:

Item Paid St Mildred's pporcon (proportion) of expenses. Endeavouring to gett the Spire built on the Steeple £7. 0. 7[2]

---

[1] Vestry Minutes St Stephen, 1648–1699, Guildhall Library.
[2] *History of St Mildred Poultry* by Thos. Milbourn, 1872, p. 81. As a matter of fact, the tower obviously was not designed for a spire, though a small bell cage was added.

THREE

The Churches of Sir Christopher Wren: Exteriors and Interiors

THE TOWERS

The remarkable variety and beauty of Wren's churches derive from a combination of his own inventive genius with close study of the work of Inigo Jones, and of Roman and Renaissance buildings as presented in the numerous architectural handbooks and copybooks coming into England from Italy, France and the Low Countries – also from personal observation in France where he spent nine months in 1664.

Wren's designs combined elements from many and varied sources and his towers and spires constituted the first and in many cases the finest of the long line of Classical steeples that graced London and the whole country during the following 120 years.

The necessity for economy and the hemmed-in sites led Wren to restrict his ornament mostly to the upper parts of the towers, and unless better placed than usual the bodies of the churches are frequently plain to the point of bareness.

The numerous drawings – 'Studies for Churches' – remaining at All Souls' College, Oxford and King's Topographical Collections, British Museum,[1] establish that Wren produced, as time went on, a considerable stock-in-trade of architectural forms suitable for application to his varied exteriors and interiors. This was especially so with his tower-finishings.

Thus among the drawings for St Antholin's steeple are two with a domical crown – these were discarded for a stone spire, and one of the dome designs was used for St Benet, Paul's Wharf. And a pagoda-like erection of diminishing temples that first appears on the cupola of Wren's earlier, 'Warrant', design for St Paul's and also found in a most inelegant form on St Magnus steeple, eventually materialized as St Bride's beautiful spire. Where, in several cases, an alternative form is shown, the steeple actually built is nearly always an improvement on it, and sometimes, as we have seen, Wren had models made.[2] All these things demonstrate his care in designing these buildings.

In considering Wren's towers it must be remembered that the Renaissance steeple had never been seen in England before, and that he built not a dozen or so but half a hundred of them, no two of which were alike and to which he gave far greater variety than was present in their pre-Fire counterparts. They range from absolute plainness to much magnificence (Bow Church, St Bride and Christ Church) and include among other ornaments

---

[1] Reproduced in Vols IX & X of the Wren Society.
[2] As £5.15.0d. to Thomas Heisenbuttle for a model for the spire or tower of Christ Church. It was very unusual for Wren to employ foreigners; *Archaeologia* Vol 66 (1914–15) p. 6.

38

Note: 18 is from print of c. 1715.

DIAGRAMS OF THE CHURCH TOWERS AND SPIRES OF SIR CHR. WREN IN LONDON. GIVEN AS

Note: 19 & 23 from
Maitland's Hist, 1756,
also 39a

...IBLE IN THEIR ORIGINAL STATE

For key see pages 40–41

a variety of urns which, combined with scrolls or pedestals, form beautiful pinnacles: as at Bow Church, St Paul's western towers and St Andrew, Holborn. Moreover, although the majority of his belfry windows are severely plain they include a number of notable designs as at St Andrew, Holborn (very elaborate), St Nicholas Cole Abbey and formerly St Benet Gracechurch (combined with pediments), St Benet Fink (oval), and St Mildred, Poultry (without dripstone or sill and framed in a sunk panel). Two have triple belfry openings (Christ Church and St Peter, Cornhill), and one had a similar arrangement above the bells and forming an open storey (All Hallows, Bread Street).

In one case, St Mary-le-Bow, the louvre boards were shaped after the manner of an old-fashioned china-cupboard shelf – a feature missing from the present louvres.

The following classification is an attempt to make a rational and typical arrangement of Wren's steeples. Also see pp. 38–9.

1.　*Plain towers – all except No. 1 with pierced parapet*
    1.　St Matthew (brick)
    2.　All Hallows-the-Great and ⎫
    3.　All Hallows, Lombard Street ⎬ stone
    4.　St Clement Eastcheap (brick with stone quoins stuccoed over)
    5.　St Andrew-by-the-Wardrobe (brick with stone quoins, spoilt by Victorian tinkering now removed)

2.　*Towers with parapets enriched with urns, pineapples, obelisks and in one instance open arches (all stone)*
    6.　St George, Botolph Lane
    7.　St Andrew, Holborn
    8.　St Olave Jewry
    9.　All Hallows, Bread Street
   10.　St Christopher
   11.　St Mary Somerset
   12.　St Bartholomew-by-the-Exchange.

3.　*Towers with bell-cages or turrets (lead covered)*
   13.　St Mildred, Poultry
   14.　St Dionis
   15.　St Anne and St Agnes

   16.　St Stephen, Coleman Street
   17.　St Mary Aldermanbury[1]
   18.　St Clement Danes[2]
   19.　St Mary-at-Hill[3]
   20.　St Michael Bassishaw

4.　*Towers with turrets on spreading bases*
   21.　St Benet Fink (lead)
   22.　St Benet, Paul's Wharf (lead)
   23.　St Michael, Wood Street[4] (lead)
   24.　St Mary Magdalen (stone)

5.　*Towers with elaborations of the turret*
   25.　St Michael Royal (stone)
   26.　St James Garlickhithe (stone)
   27.　St Stephen Walbrook (stone)
   28.　St Paul's western towers (stone)
   29.　St Michael, Crooked Lane (lead)
These lead naturally to:

6.　*Towers with built-up spires (stone)*
   30.　St Vedast
   31.　Christ Church
   32.　St Mary-le-Bow
   33.　St Bride
Except that they fall into this category, they are utterly unlike each other.

7.　*Towers with true spires*
   34.　St Antholin (stone)
   35.　St Margaret Pattens (lead) and obelisks from class 2
   36.　St Swithun (lead)

8.　*Towers with octagonal trumpet-shaped spires (lead)*
   37.　St Edmund
   38.　St Nicholas Cole Abbey

8A.　*Towers with spires of hybrid design (lead)*
   39.　St Lawrence Jewry – classes 3 and 9 and obelisks from class 2
   39a.　St Anne, Soho – classes 4 and 5
   40.　St Augustine – classes 5 and 9 and obelisks from class 2

[1] [2] [3] [4] As left by Wren.

9. *Towers with built-up spires, concave in outline (lead)*
    41. St Michael Queenhithe
    42. St Mildred, Bread Street
    43. St Mary Abchurch
    44. St Margaret, Lothbury
    45. St Benet Gracechurch
    46. St Peter, Cornhill
    47. St Martin, Ludgate
These again are all very different.

10. *One tower with lantern, dome and spire*
    48. St Magnus

Gothic Towers (all stone):

11. *With pinnacles*
    49. St Alban
    50. St Mary Aldermary[1]
    51. St Michael, Cornhill (Hawksmoor)

12. *One tower with spire on arches*
    52. St Dunstan-in-the-East[2]

The following are, or were, the most notable:

1. *Plain towers*
All Hallows-the-Great must have been impressive from its massiveness, while St Andrew-by-the-Wardrobe is unusual with stone pilaster strips at the corners of the belfry stage, and rustication below.

2. *Towers with enriched parapets*
All interesting.

St George, Botolph Lane, a small though massive tower with boldly designed vases.

St Andrew, Holborn, a good tower with fine belfry windows – the most elaborate by Wren – and pinnacles composed of urns set on scrolled pedestals and carrying vanes, latter now removed.

St Olave Jewry, a slightly tapering tower with tall obelisks – according to Niven, Wren's only battered tower.

All Hallows, Bread Street had a superb tower with a unique arcaded top storey, the keystones of which were beautifully sculptured, and most elegant tall, carved pinnacles.

St Christopher, largely mediaeval, Wren's upper part carrying pineapples between octagonal obelisks bearing vanes.

St Mary Somerset [19], a remarkable tower, little known or appreciated, and often dismissed by critics – Birch, Stratton and Bumpus – as more curious than beautiful. A line of windows, alternately round-headed and circular, runs up the centre of each side (of which three stood free of the church), and these lines, as it were, shoot up above the parapets in tall obelisks set on pedestals, forming a diagonal arrangement, while at the corners, similar pedestals support elongated urns. All these are beautifully panelled and on a sunny day about noon look like carved ivory, while earlier, with the morning sun full on them, they resemble cream-coloured fingers thrusting up into the blue. When seen from various angles, they present remarkably different effects.

St Bartholomew-by-the-Exchange, also very remarkable, but very different from the last. On the parapet in the centre of each side was an open arch[3] supported by ramps leaving the corners unadorned – this, at the time of demolition in 1841 – but Maitland, in his *History of London*, 1756, shows pedestals there – did they ever support obelisks? In any case a charming, though whimsical design. But contemporaries unkindly say that the arches gave the tower the appearance of being in process of demolition!

3. *Towers with bell-turrets*
These do not call for much comment, except to say that the turrets themselves vary more in size than any other class of steeple, from the tiny bell-cage at St Mildred, Poultry to the very large erection at St Michael Bassishaw, and that all were pleasing.

The tower of St Clement Danes, before Gibbs made his addition, is shown in a print of about 1715 with a short massive turret, with smaller ones at the corners to which it is connected by curved iron rods – curious flying buttresses! The tower itself is mediaeval, remodelled by Wren who transformed the original buttresses into engaged obelisks.

[1] Top of these pinnacles originally a ball and vane.
[2] All this variety of design could not have been translated into fact but for Wren's engineering skill.
[3] Some engravings show them filled with louvre boards.

17   St Clement, Eastcheap

18   St Andrew, Holborn

19 St Mary Somerset: Baroque pinnacles

20 & 21   All Hallows, Bread Street and St Benet Fink from drawings by W. Niven, 1887

4. *Steeples of three different designs, similar in outline* St Benet Fink [21] and St Benet, Paul's Wharf [22] both have domes, but whereas the latter is circular and supports a beautiful lantern, the former was square in plan and carried a bell-cage surmounted by a ball and cross – seemingly the only example among Wren's parish churches of a cross being used instead of a vane.[1] The belfry windows of this church were also unique, being oval, with swags below, while above, the cornice swept over them in a graceful curve. The other St Benet has a brick

_____

[1] That on St Mary Abchurch spire is Victorian.

22   St Benet, Paul's Wharf

23   St Mary Magdalen, Old Fish Street

tower with stone quoins and the beautiful proportions of the cupola and lantern with their contrasting curves help to make this little steeple a work of
art that is quite perfect.[1]

At St Michael, Wood Street, the curved pyramid
supporting the lantern, with the little roof of the
same shape above,[2] must have made a pleasing

composition. It was replaced about 1804 by a dull-
looking spire.

The one stone example, at St Mary Magdalen,
was a really charming design with a lantern on five

---

[1] Except for the rather clumsy vane – probably a renewal.
[2] Taken from Maitland.

24   St Michael, Paternoster Royal

25   St James Garlickhithe

octagonal steps and bearing a vase instead of the usual ball and vane. Its destruction was a great loss.

5.   *Elaboration of the bell-turret*

On the tower of St Michael, Crooked Lane was a remarkable lead-covered erection of three circular stages with arches and ramps forming

buttresses at the diagonals and terminating in a finial like a gigantic baluster or Indian club.[1] Although destroyed as long ago as 1831, there are

---

[1] The several stages were originally adorned with lead vases, but they were removed in 1756 by order of the vestry, as they had become dangerous (*History of St Michael, Crooked Lane*).

26   St Stephen Walbrook: spire and dome

many views of it – it occurs again and again in the beautiful drawings by E.W. Cooke, R.A., of the demolition of Old London Bridge (in the Guildhall). It must have been a beautiful design.

Of those in stone, the three parochial examples are, at first sight, much alike, and are composed of diminishing storeys, the lowest pillared, adorned

with urns; but on plan they are all different. That at St Stephen Walbrook [26] which is larger in proportion to the tower than the other two, is square on plan with extra columns projecting at the corners.

St James's is also square on plan, but with two columns placed diagonally at the corners and supporting bold scrolled ramps.

At St Michael Royal [24] the plan is octagonal with eight pillars over which the entablature breaks in horizontal battlements. These two steeples can be seen from the same point in Thames Street, and it is interesting to note how Wren has varied the details.

It may seem almost irreverent to place such magnificent structures as the bell towers of St Paul's in this category, but they are essentially the same kind of steeple. They are wonderfully designed with convex, concave and circular stages, and constitute the finest examples of the English equivalent of Baroque. Rich and solid-looking from some views, if seen diagonally from a distance they appear like fretwork, the voids almost equalling the solids. The ornaments at the corners of the clock stage, helping to lead the eye to the steeple proper, are really lovely and consist of urns supported by intricate scrollwork ending in lion's claws.

6. *Built-up spires*

With this class, the climax of beauty is reached and each tower in it is unique in some respect.

St Vedast [30] is a most graceful and original design, and unusual in having no vases but relying for its effect on the play of light and shade on contrasting surfaces and cornices – concave and convex – with strongly emphasized angles.

Christ Church is square throughout, and its three-fold louvred openings on each side are echoed by the colonnade above, which was formerly crowned by 12 urns whose removal, before 1814, spoiled the steeple but by private benefaction new urns were erected in 1959. The position of the lower vases is unusual and the finial was very delicate.[1]

---

[1] Marred in the rebuilding by, apparently, cutting off the stone tip and bringing down the lead work of the vane to cover its place.

27 St Mary-le-Bow from Birch's *London Churches*, 1896

28 Christ Church, Newgate Street, as restored in 1958–59

At St Mary-le-Bow is what can reasonably be regarded as the perfect Renaissance steeple. Its finely designed belfry-storey, open-work corner pinnacles of rare beauty, circular peristyle, flying-buttressed above against the central (staircase) shaft which supports the pillared and spired finial,

all betoken Wren's genius. The great dragon-vane, 8 feet in length, is one of the supporters of the City Arms, in unfamiliar position.

St Bride, Wren's tallest, is in some ways the opposite of Bow steeple, for whereas the latter is all elegance, leading the eye easily from stage to

29   St Bride, Fleet Street from the west

30   St Vedast, Foster Lane

stage, the former with its repeated motif of diminishing arcades is an essay in considered breaks – steps forming a rigid, but none the less beautiful spire.[1] Though perhaps in theory a doubtful architectural expedient, Wren has 'brought it off', and therein lies his justification. The belfry

stage is beautifully designed and the whole steeple tower and spire together, forms a perfect unity. It was struck by lightning in 1764 and the upper

---

[1] The stages are not identical – all have varied bases, while the fourth is quite distinctive and formerly supported eight urns.

31   St Antholin, demolished 1876, from a drawing by
W. Niven, etched 1884

32   St Margaret Pattens

part rebuilt by Sir W. Staines, who, it is said,
shortened the whole height by 8 feet, but it is
hard to see how, for its proportions are not spoiled,
as one would imagine if lowered by 8 feet.

7.   *True Spires*

The solitary stone example, at St Antholin, was
a very fine design, and its removal was a disgrace.
Below the spire and forming the connection
between it and the square tower, was an octagonal
belfry stage with, on the diagonal faces, semi-

33   St Swithun, Cannon Street

1820s, was removed, and somehow found its way into a garden at Forest Hill where it still stands over a well, but in altered surroundings.

On the demolition of the church in 1875, it was at first proposed to retain the tower. Drawings are extant showing how it was to have been 'improved' so as to range with the new Queen Victoria Street – the whole of it below the spire would have been covered with ornament. But, as if in response to a guilty conscience, a memorial to the church was erected at the corner of Sise Lane and Budge Row, bombed in the last war and long since removed. But the centre piece, with a very good relief of the church, was saved, and is now in St Mary Aldermary.

The two lead-covered spires St Swithun, Cannon Street (now destroyed) and St Margaret Pattens [32] were really mediaeval in spirit, especially the former where the lead was laid longitudinally – the latter has bands forming sunk panels – and both were pierced at intervals. St Swithun rose from within an octagonal balustraded parapet, to receive which the corners of the tower were scooped off – a curious but not unattractive expedient. At St Margaret the tower, much higher than St Swithun's, is square to the top, and has tall stone pinnacles tipped with lead and scrolled at their base, connected by a fine balustrade, above which the spire rises to a height of nearly 200 feet. Lead vases, once half way up, have long been removed.[1] Altogether a simple and noble structure.

8.   Towers with trumpet-shaped spires
These two almost whimsical erections were scorned by Godwin, who calls one 'ugly' and the other 'more Chinese than English'. But they were not without charm.

At St Nicholas [35], the shorter of the two, the tower, now rebuilt, had fine belfry windows crowned above the cornice with pediments, but there was no parapet. At the corners stood four rather plain-looking vases, and from within these the slightly curved octagonal spire rose from a low base and sustained a cornice and balcony with a pedestal bearing a curious bottle-shaped orna-

circular buttresses with domical tops. The spire itself was panelled and had a series of eight pedimented windows at its base, with pierced cartouches and shells higher up, and terminated rather curiously in a composite capital carrying the vane. The upper third of the spire, on its renewal, it is said, in the

---

[1] In 1975 there were plans to replace these, but they were abandoned for lack of money.

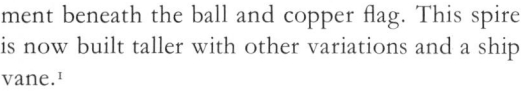
34 St Edmund, Lombard Street before the urns were removed from the steeple

35 St Nicholas Cole Abbey (pre-war)

ment beneath the ball and copper flag. This spire is now built taller with other variations and a ship vane.[1]

St Edmund's [34] is much loftier and more tapering than the last and rests upon an eight-sided base with as many shouldered windows; above the

angles were eight flaming urns with four more half way up the spire, all twelve shamefully removed about the turn of the century. Here the cornice makes a much smaller platform than at St Nicholas

---

[1] See Guide.

36 St Lawrence Jewry

37 St Augustine, Watling Street, showing new spire of 1966

and directly bears the finial. On the parapet of the tower are pineapples and vases.

8A. *Towers with spires of hybrid design*

At St Lawrence Jewry [36] upon a tower (not square) with obelisk pinnacles is a simple steeple

composed entirely of straight lines except for the arched openings on each side. These latter are crowned with pediments and resemble four projecting portals – a motif Wren used on two other occasions, at St Stephen, Coleman Street (a bell turret covered with a curved and pointed roof), and St Benet Gracechurch, to be noticed shortly.

At St Lawrence Jewry is a short spire bearing a vane in the form of a gridiron.

At St Anne, Soho was a remarkable design. Within a parapet with lowered corners, bearing urns, rose an octagonal dome sustaining an open, balustrated temple, having an elaborate roof merging by concave and ogee curves on to the finial. This steeple was replaced by the present curious one by S.P. Cockerell, 1802–6.

At St Augustine [37] the tower is oblong in plan and has an almost Jacobean pierced parapet with pinnacles carved with scrolls and masks, and supporting an elaborate and graceful composition with urns and topped by an enormous Indian club-like finial – as at St Michael, Crooked Lane. St Augustine's outline was spoiled when the part above the urns was rebuilt straight (in 1829–30), but the original design was restored when the spire was reinstated in 1966.

9. *Built-up lead-covered spires*
These are very slender and exhibit great variety of design; and each consists above the tower of three stages, a domical or other spreading base, a bell-cage and the spire proper.[1]

At St Michael Queenhithe the latter was raised above five steps and had a notable vane in the form of a ship under sail, made in the round and said to be capable of holding a bushel of grain. This was for many years to be seen above a miniature spire on the site of the church; it now forms the vane of St Nicholas Cole Abbey.

At St Mildred, Bread Street the base was made of four concave surfaces which led gracefully up to the tall obelisk spire with a heraldic and monogrammatic vane.

At St Margaret, Lothbury [39], the tower is lofty and the spire square, small but very elegant, and raised on a cupola of the same plan but bell-shaped in outline, banded midway and set with four deep eyes.

St Mary Abchurch has a very simple steeple, square throughout. The spire and arched openings for the bell stand on an ogee dome, leading the eye easily from the tower to the finial (now a cross) in one graceful curve.[2]

At St Benet Gracechurch was a combination of

38   St Mildred, Bread Street

dome and spire (square plan) with between them the arrangement of four porticoes mentioned above.

---

[1] Except St Margaret, Lothbury which has no bell-cage.

[2] The spire proper has been rebuilt. Formerly it had small panels at the base with corner scrolls and a flag vane, but this displaced the original vane, a pelican on its nest, now in the church.

39   St Margaret, Lothbury

40   St Peter, Cornhill

The upper part of the tower had inset corners and fine belfry windows under large pediments giving the whole steeple a most distinguished appearance.

The brick tower of St Peter, Cornhill [40] is exceptional with its 12 arched windows (louvred) and series of cornices (reminiscent of an Italian campanile), and it sustains a beautiful composition of dome and octagonal lantern and spire. The finial, which is disfigured by modern direction indicators, has a large key for a vane – symbol of the patron St Peter.

St Martin, Ludgate [41] the most successful perhaps of all, is remarkable for the masterly way the transition from the massive tower to the

41   St Martin, Ludgate

10.   *Steeple of St Magnus*

This fine design with its octagonal domed temple and 'spiry turret', is evidently inspired by a large Wren-period elevation in the Soane Collection, of the very Baroque tower and steeple of St Charles Borromée, at Antwerp[1] – built in 1614–24 by François Aiguillon, s.j. Comparison of photographs of these two towers shows close resemblance of outline, but amazing difference of ornamentation – a good example of Wren's improvement on his original.

All but the top of St Magnus steeple is now partly boxed in by Adelaide House. Its full former dignity, as it stood guard over old London Bridge until 1831, was seen for a short time before the aforesaid house was built in 1924.

Gothic Towers:

11.   *With pinnacles*

These three examples are quite different in other respects.

St Alban, a fine sturdy tower now isolated in the middle of Wood Street, has double belfry windows with good tracery, and had a fine corona of pinnacles but unfortunately these and the parapet were renewed last century in a darker stone, spoiling it completely.

At St Mary Aldermary the slender tower with pronounced octagonal corner turrets beautifully panelled[2] is mediaeval – Sir Henry Keeble's work – in the lower part, which Wren repaired, carried up and crowned with tall pinnacles of ogee outline ending in balls and vanes, later altered to slender foliaged finials. These latter were renewed, wider than before, in Victorian times, but were removed as unsafe about 1927 and, broken up, they helped to make a rockery in the burial ground. The pinnacles now bear foliaged finials in fibre-glass.

The tower of St Michael, Cornhill, often men-

octagonal superstructure is managed and the way the curious ogee 'dome' leads up gracefully through the balcony – a happy thought – to the fine lantern and spire that is such a contrast to the swelling form of St Paul's.

---

[1] Wren Society, Vol xii, pl. 32 – where it is unrecognized but see also Seckler, p. 80 and note.

[2] There is a remarkable resemblance between these turrets and those in a drawing of a proposed campanile for King's College Chapel, Cambridge, among the Cotton MSS. at the British Museum (reproduced in Lyson's *Cambridgeshire*, 1808 p. 116). St Mary's tower was begun by Keeble in 1510 and as the panelling of the turrets, identical with that in the drawing seems otherwise to be unique, they surely must have had a common origin?

42 & 43   The steeples of St Charles Borromée, Antwerp, built 1614–24 by François Aiguillon, and Wren's St Magnus, built 1703–06

44 Design (never built) for a campanile for King's
College, Cambridge from an engraving in Lyson's
Cambridgeshire, 1808

45 St Mary Aldermary (before body of church was
'improved' in 1876), showing finials of 1765. From a
photograph in *The Portfolio* of 1871

46   St Michael Cornhill

47   St Dunstan-in-the-East

tioned as Wren's last work, finished in 1721, is now attributed to Hawksmoor.[1] Certainly, as built, it is unlike the two drawings of a Gothic tower for St Michael's, one signed by Dickinson and the other with 'Sir C. Wren' on the back. The massive corner turrets end in pinnacles set back, panelled and crocketted, bearing foliaged finials with sharp spikes (formerly vaned) and decorated with carved heads alternately young and old. Altogether it is a very stately tower of which no good view from the ground can be obtained.

12.   *St Dunstan-in-the-East*

This fine steeple, inspired we may suppose by that of old Bow Church, is well known with its tall pinnacles within which the needle-like spire is held aloft on slender flying buttresses. Note also the weather-cock, unusual for Wren. Of the tower, noteworthy points are the charming ground storey

---

[1] Summerson, *Architecture in Britain* 1530–1830, Seckler, *Wren and his Place in European Architecture*, and Kerry Downes, *Hawksmoor*, 1969.

with its dome and outside ironwork, and the window tracery.

This provokes a word as to those delightful finials to Wren's steeples. They usually consist of a rod bearing a ball and vane, generally in the form of a pennon with sometimes an intermediate ornament; at St Augustine and St Margaret Pattens this was a kind of daisy bud with spreading or curled tips to the petals; at St Benet, Paul's Wharf, a flat disk below a leaf-bud, and at St Nicholas Cole Abbey, four S's back to back. Sometimes an extra ball was added, and there is generally some delicate ironwork on the counterpoise of the vane, and in some cases the whole finial is topped with a cross or a crown.

The following is a list of special vanes and finials:

St Lawrence Jewry	Gridiron – emblem of the patron saint
St Peter, Cornhill	Key – emblem of the patron saint
St Mary Abchurch	Pelican-in-its-Piety (massive original now in the church)
St Mary-le-Bow	Dragon – supporters of City Arms
St Michael Queenhithe	Ship (in the round) now at St Nicholas Cole Abbey
St Mildred, Poultry	Ship (cut out) now at St Olave Jewry (re-made?)
St Mary Aldermanbury	Comet
St Dunstan-in-the-East	Peacock (called a 'cock' in building accounts)
St Stephen, Coleman Street	Cock[1]
St Swithun	Formerly a phoenix
St Mildred, Bread Street	Armorial and monogrammatic (The monogram was two B's and an M, and the arms those of Crispe)
St Anne and St Agnes	The vane is topped with a large 'A' and the counterpoise ends in what appears to be a griffin's head
St Andrew, Holborn St Christopher	Square flag-vanes on pinnacles
St Michael, Cornhill	Has spikes but formerly the tower bore comet[2] vanes
St Benet Fink, Tower	A cross instead of vane
At St Mary Magdalen	A copper urn instead of a vane[3]

THE EXTERIORS

Wren's exteriors, quite apart from the towers, varied tremendously according to site and plan. Some few, like St Bride were symmetrical throughout, with a tower projecting at the centre of the west end. But in most cases the tower was placed at the north-west or south-west corner, and either end or side of the church made the principal façade according to the position of the street.

The most usual treatment of the sides was to have a series of uniform windows, with generally a door at the west end. The finest example of this arrangement was perhaps at St Michael Queenhithe where each bay consisted of a round-headed window with a circular one above, to which it was connected by a scrolled keystone and swags. Crowning the whole was a winged cherub's head. Other notable 'broadsides' were at St Mary Magdalen (where the circular-headed windows were flanked by rich brackets), St Nicholas Cole Abbey, St Benet Fink (ten sided, and in those free of buildings a large mullioned window beneath festoons), and St Benet, Paul's Wharf [22], a really charming exterior of red brick with stone quoins and round-headed windows surmounted by richly carved swags in high relief, while above, over the north aisle, three hipped roofs add to the picturesque effect.

Occasionally the sides are treated as a symmetrical composition as at St Mildred, Poultry, St Swithun,

---

[1] Part of the parish device of a cock and hoop, occurring on a paten of 1630, the beadle's staff 1736, and a carved sign on a house in Coleman Street belonging to the parish dated 1754. Hatton says a figure of a cock was carved under the pediment on the east end of the church.

[2] See Churchwardens Committee Book, Guildhall Library MS4073/1 20.4.1752.

[3] St Paul's Lib., W.D.37.

48   The south side of St Michael Queenhithe

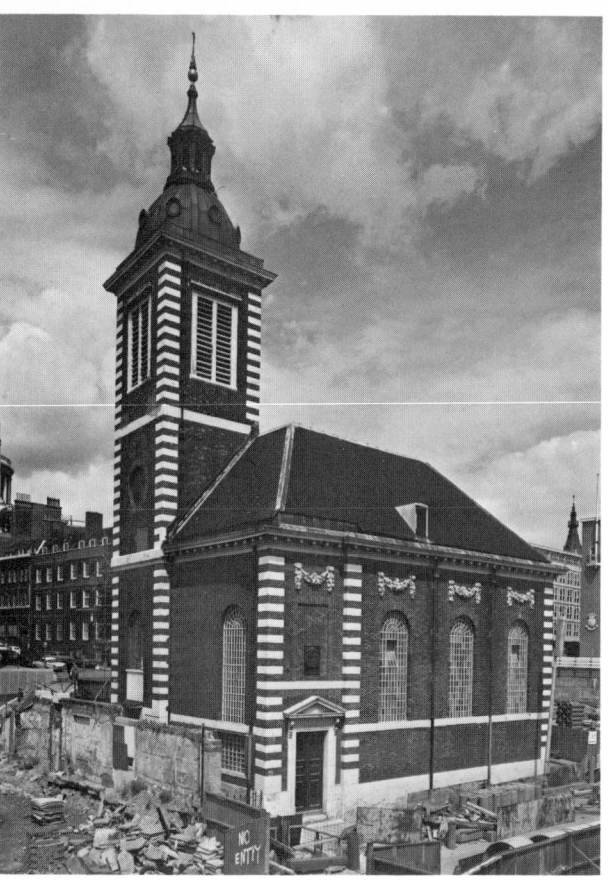

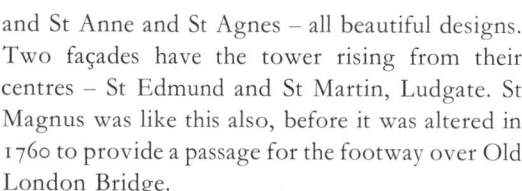

49   St Benet, Paul's Wharf, from the south-west

50   St Swithun, Cannon Street, before 1869 (when the windows received plate tracery)

and St Anne and St Agnes – all beautiful designs. Two façades have the tower rising from their centres – St Edmund and St Martin, Ludgate. St Magnus was like this also, before it was altered in 1760 to provide a passage for the footway over Old London Bridge.

The best examples of west fronts with towers at the sides occur at St Clement Eastcheap, St Margaret Pattens, and St Vedast – all very plain, though the last has an unusual 'Venetian' central window. At St Mildred, Bread Street, the tower was placed at the east end of the south side, leaving the west front free; at All Hallows-the-Great it was near the east end of the north aisle, while at St Mary-le-Bow the steeple is separated from the west end by a spacious vestibule.

The finest east end is at St Lawrence Jewry,

a very beautiful composition. Other good examples are, or were, at St Peter, Cornhill [52], St Dionis Backchurch, St Mary Aldermanbury (before alteration), St Mary-at-Hill, St Michael, Wood Street, and St Matthew.

Wren's doorways are generally unpretentious, though there are some notable exceptions, especially the splendid portals of Bow church tower, among the finest this side of Italy. At St Bride (west door), St Margaret, Lothbury (a porch), St Stephen Walbrook (with an oval window above), and formerly at St Benet Fink, are, or were, other good examples. A simple but unusual doorway occurs at St Clement Eastcheap – semi-circular with plain concave mouldings. And in the southern face of Bow church tower (leading from the vestibule) is a vast doorway with a concave arch and

51 The east end of St
Lawrence Jewry

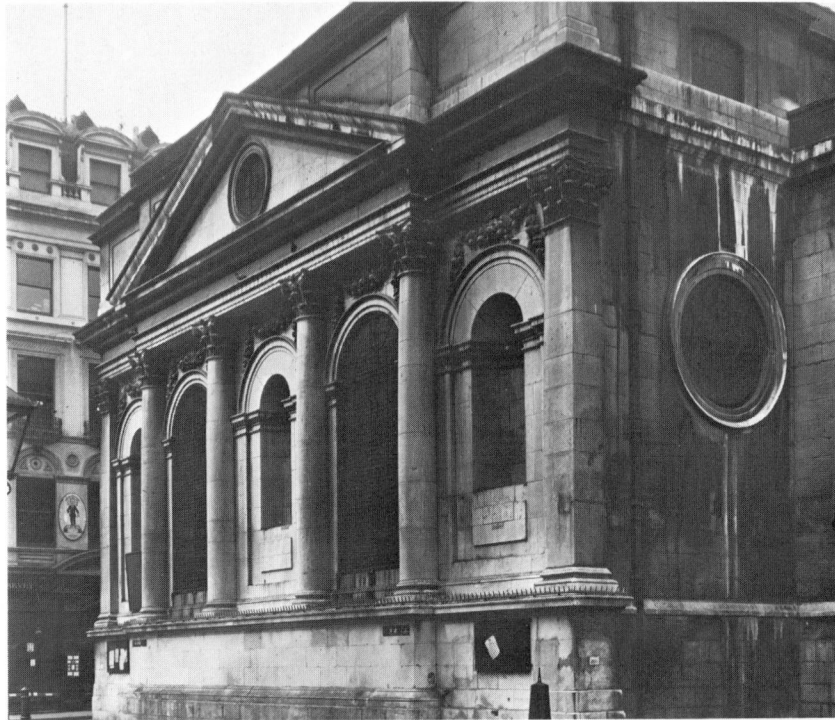

52 The east end of St
Peter, Cornhill

53   The east end of St Dionis Backchurch

54 The west door-
ways of St Magnus

55 Top of north
entrance to the tower,
St Mary-le-Bow

56   One of four fine
doorways, St Martin,
Ludgate

57   All Hallows,
Lombard Street,
showing south-west
doorway now at
Twickenham

58 Door to rector's room, St Mary Abchurch. Note former weathervane above

jambs (which are continuous), very striking by its size and simplicity. Also, St Clement Danes has a charming west porch.

CLOCKS

A conspicuous feature of many of the exteriors was the often very elaborate projecting clock. Originally pretty numerous, as a glance at Toms' engravings, 1736–39, and the illustrations to

Maitland's *History of London*, 1756, will show, they tended as time went on to be replaced by plainer ones, as at St Swithun and St Olave, Hart Street, or by mere wall clocks as at St Mildred, Poultry. Formerly there were fine examples of the early rich type at old St Dunstan-in-the-West,[1] St Mildred, Poultry, St Olave, Hart Street, St Peter-le-Poer (in the centre of a beam over the road), and St Stephen, Coleman Street, and over the river, at old St Olave, Tooley Street. The only ones remaining in 1940 were at All Hallows, Barking, St James Garlickhithe,[2] St Mary-le-Bow, St Mary-at-Hill, and St Magnus, and of these the last two — now the only survivors — were also the finest. But that at St Magnus was once still more splendid as the following description in Hatton's *New View of London* shows:

'The Church, which was new beautified 1705 and 1706, is adorned on the outside with a Doorcase of the *Ionick* Order and a curious Dial having the Figures of Atlas and Hercules, St Magnus and St Margaret,[3] and 2 Cupids, 1 with a Sun and the other holding an Hour-glass as also two eagles and several Cherubim. The 2 first Figures are very spacious and lye on the Pediment of the West Door-case, the rest are erect, richly carved and gilt'.[4]

The old clock at Bow church dated 1682 must have been equally fine.

SUNDIALS

Examples survive at St Katherine Cree (very elaborate with date, 1706, and motto *Non Sine Lumine*), and at St Sepulchre. St Clement Danes had both a clock and a sundial. In 1671 payment was made to 'Mr Wynn, the Mathematician, for designing twoo sunn dyalls on the Church wall' of £1 15s. od. He was also paid 'for Designing the Clock Dyall on the out side of the Steeple, £1 7s. od.'

---

[1] This was accompanied by the famous striking figures set up in 1671 which, after a sojourn of 100 years in Regent's Park, are now back in Fleet Street.

[2] The crude statue of St James was formerly between two urns.

[3] St Margaret, New Fish Street, was not rebuilt after 1666, the parish being united to St Magnus.

[4] 'Sir Charles Duncombe gave in 1700 £484 5s. 4d. charge of Clock and Dial' (Hatton).

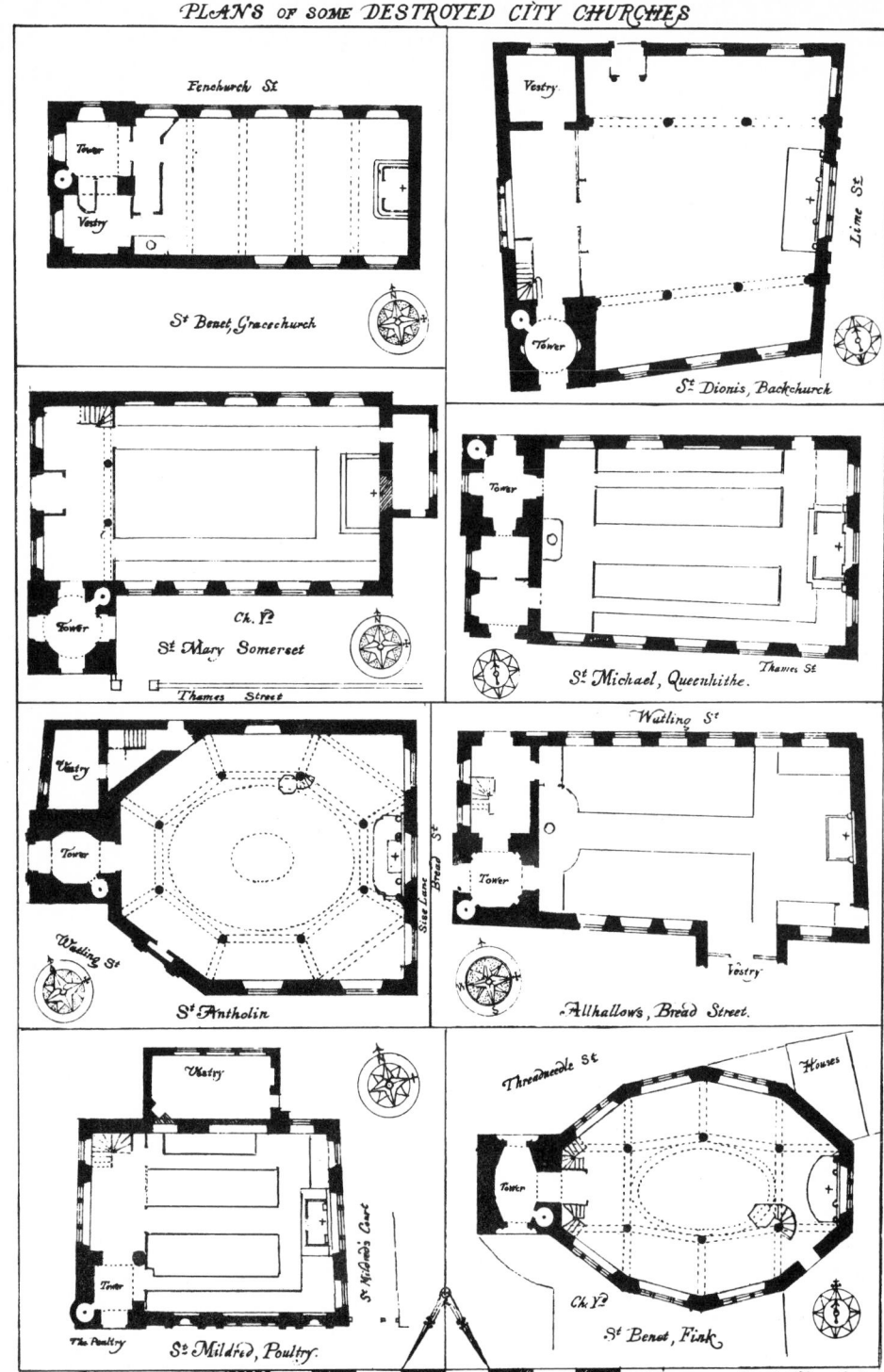

PLANS OF SOME DESTROYED CITY CHURCHES

59   Plans of eight Wren City churches, drawn by W. Niven *c.*1887

But this was on the pre-Wren church. The present dial occupies a carved and pedimented frame, which formerly contained the clock.[1] In the same print two sundials together are shown higher up at the south-west angle of the tower.

INTERIORS

With his interiors Wren was particularly successful, and considering he had to conform his plans to every variety of site, resulting in churches rectangular (from square to narrow oblong), irregular (St Stephen, Coleman Street etc.), coffin-shaped (St Olave, Old Jewry), and angular oval (St Benet Fink), it increases one's admiration for his ingenuity and judgment. One may arrange his interiors in six categories:

1. Plain rooms, more or less rectangular
2. Plain rooms with one aisle
3. Nave and aisles
4. Ditto, with apse (one example only – St Clement Danes)
5. Rectangular, with internal cruciform arrangement
6. Angular ovals with pillars and aisle

Over these he placed, either singly or in combination, one or more of the following classes of ceiling (all in plaster):

1. Flat roofs
2. Flat roofs, supported by a cove
3. Semi-circular, segmental or elliptical barrel vaults
4. Groined vaults
5. Domes

PLAIN ROOMS AND WITH ONE AISLE

Over classes 1 and 2 of the list, Wren usually placed flat roofs with a wide cove, which was generally groined over the windows. All Hallows, Lombard Street, was a noble example of this simple treatment. The central flat part was in most cases enriched with panels and beautiful wreaths of fruit and flowers, as at St Vedast and St Clement Eastcheap. In one instance, St Michael, Wood Street, the cove was north and south only, the wreathed central panel coming right up to the east and west walls, and at St Benet Gracechurch, a narrow plan [59], there was a groined vault with enriched traverse arches.

Of the few main ceilings that were flat without coves, those at St Benet, Paul's Wharf, and St Nicholas, Cole Abbey were the only survivors. The former is perfectly plain, except for the entablature and cornice at the top of the walls, supported by Corinthian pilasters and pillars, but the latter was divided into compartments by broad moulded beams.

NAVES AND AISLES

Of class 3, the basilican type, many varieties occur, and include Wren's two Gothic interiors – St Alban and St Mary Aldermary.

In one case (St Bartholomew-by-the-Exchange) a flat roof was employed for both nave and aisles, but for the former, in most cases, a barrel vault was used, though sometimes as at Christ Church and St Stephen Walbrook a groined vault with enriched transverse arches. The aisles were generally groined, but at St James, Piccadilly there were small barrel vaults, rising from an entablature, at right angles to the main axis.

The division between nave and aisles was of three kinds: columns and entablature (Christ Church, St Dionis Backchurch etc.), pillars and arches (St Bride, St Peter, Cornhill etc.), and pillars supporting the arch-like intersection of a groined aisle roof with a main barrel vault (St Andrew-by-the-Wardrobe and St Andrew, Holborn).[2] In the latter case there were no clerestory windows, the aisles being kept lofty for the introduction of a gallery. But otherwise Wren nearly always introduced upper windows of some kind, a notable exception being at St Peter, Cornhill, where piers and arches sustain an entablature and attic from which springs a vault slightly elliptical and divided into panels. The aisles have transverse vaults as at St James, Piccadilly, but instead of resting on entablatures they are cut into by semi-circles forming arches from pier to wall – a very unusual

---

[1] Which may very well be Mr Wynn's, as Wren only recased the old tower.
[2] At St Clement Danes an enriched band gave the impression of an arch, as also a moulded rib at St Augustine.

60   All Hallows-the-Great, Thames Street, looking east. Screen now in St Margaret Lothbury

61   St Lawrence Jewry, looking west, *c*.1907

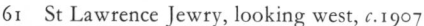

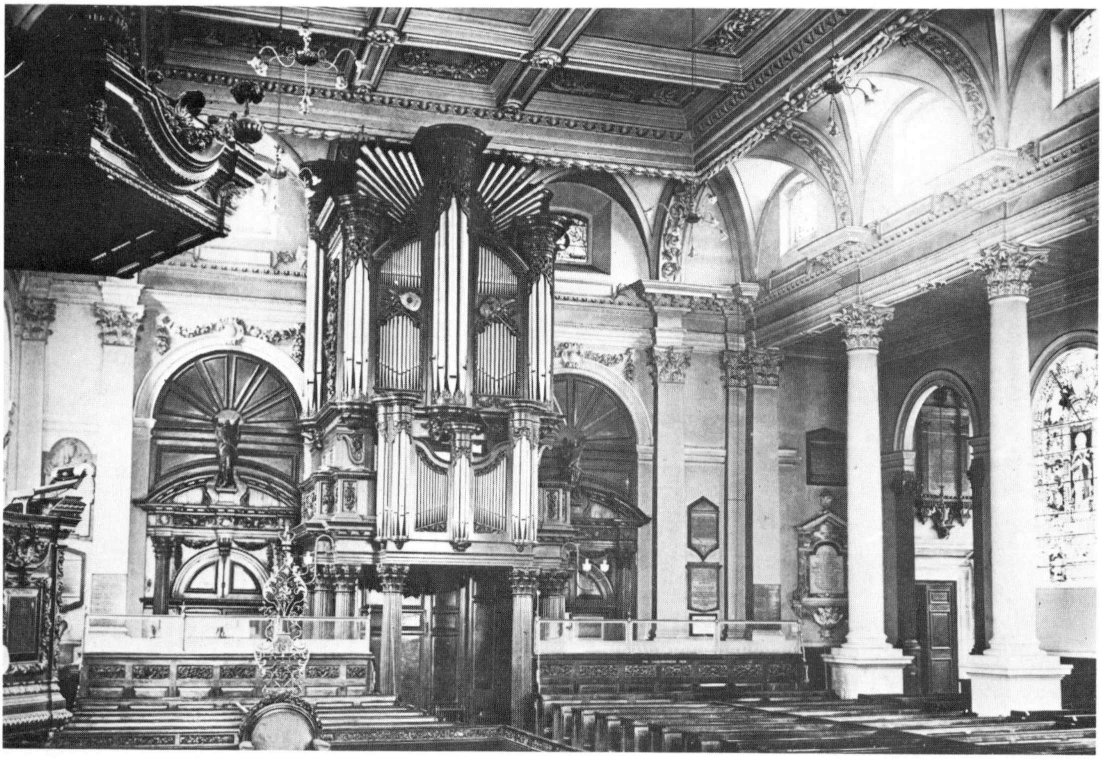

62 St Andrew Holborn, from Birch's *London Churches*, 1896

arrangement, also occurring with a variation at St Mary-le-Bow.

At St Mary Aldermanbury the semi-circular roof was interrupted midway by a groin over two large lunettes, while at St James Garlickhithe the main ceiling is flat with wide coves which spring from a cornice carried on the north and south by Ionic pillars, forming narrow aisles and stopped each side of a kind of transept – an unusual and charming interior.

St Clement Danes, though classed separately, was really only a variety of class 3. The ceilings were accommodated to a curious plan of double apses.

St Mary-le-Bow and St George, Botolph Lane, were of three bays each, the centre one on each side being wider than the others – in the latter case so much so that the plan is almost identical with the first three in class 5.

INTERNAL CRUCIFORM ARRANGEMENT (Class 5)

This applies to St Anne and St Agnes, St Martin, Ludgate, St Mary-at-Hill, and St Stephen Walbrook. In the first three the plan has a square (more or less) with four columns in the midst, supporting entablatures and crossing barrel vaults with a flat ceiling in each corner. At St Anne and St Agnes and St Martin this gives a groin at the centre, but at St Mary there is a shallow dome on pendentives.[1] It is interesting how, in each case, Wren has got an entirely different effect by varying

---

[1] This by Savage, 1826.

63 St Martin Ludgate, looking across the nave

64 St Mary-at-Hill, from Birch's *London Churches*, 1896

the proportions. At St Martin the interior is very lofty and the pillars, on high bases, are close together and bear a very rich entablature. At St Anne and St Agnes the supports are wide apart and the groin correspondingly large, while at St Mary the body of the church is oblong and the pillars are moderately spaced.

St Stephen will be described in the next class.

INTERIORS WITH DOMES (Class 6)

These are St Mildred, Bread Street [68], St Swithun, St Mary Abchurch [65], St Stephen Walbrook [66], St Antholin [67] and St Benet Fink. These, quite apart from their variety and individual beauty,

were interesting from the different ways they were supported.

At St Mildred the plan was an oblong and the dome rested on wall arches north and south, and wide arches, springing from elaborate corbels, to prolong the roof east and west. The pendentives were richly decorated, and cherubs in couples originally gave interest to the cupola – it was a lovely interior, with all its fittings unspoilt.

At St Swithun the octagonal dome sprang from an entablature of the same shape sustained on seven half columns and one whole one (which carried the north aisle roof).

At St Mary Abchurch the cupola, which is round,

65   St Mary Abchurch: the ceiling by William Snow, as restored after war damage

is held up by groined pendentives which continue its lines down to the corbels from which they spring. The arches formed by this vaulting are curiously irregular, some being slightly pointed, and others go behind the cornice they support. The dome was dark with paintings, now cleaned and repaired, and is pierced by four oval windows.

At St Stephen Walbrook, which was of course Wren's most famous interior, the elaborately panelled dome which carried a lantern, was the glory of a roof supported by 16 pillars, eight of which, bearing arches, were required by the cupola. Bumpus, in his *Ancient London Churches*, p. 392, says:

'Never was so sweet a kernel in so rough a shell. . . . The tameness of its form, a simple cell enclosed by four walls, wholly disappears behind the unique and varied arrangement of its sixteen Corinthian columns. . . . Now they form the Latin Cross, with its nave, transept and chancel; anon they divide the whole space into five aisles, regularly diminishing from the centre to the sides; again we perceive, in the midst, a square apartment with recesses on all sides – a square, nay, an octagon – no, a circle. It changes at every glance. . . . With the same harmonious variety, we have every form of ceiling brought together at once – flat, camerated, groined,

66   The dome of St Stephen Walbrook as restored after war damage

67 Painting of St
Antholin 1876, a year
after the demolition of
the church. No photo-
graph is known.

pendentive, domical – yet without any confusion
or straining after effect.'

But the effect must have been still finer before the
pews were removed and the octagonal bases altered
to the present clumsy square pedestals on the
authority of some misleading engravings of the
early eighteenth century showing the church bare
of fittings – as Loftie suggests, the whole church
seemed to rise upward from the breast-high mass
of dark oak.

The two interiors with oval domes must have
been fascinating, and their loss is a grievous one.

At St Benet Fink the restricted site forbade a
rectangular plan, so Wren designed a ten-sided
church, with projecting west tower. Within, he
disposed six pillars so as to support on as many
arches an elliptical cupola carrying a lantern, the

aisles being spanned by entablatures bearing barrel-
vaults, two running east and west and four north
and south.

At St Antholin, the plan was a rectangle with the
south-west corner cut off, so Wren repeated this
internally to form a north-west vestry, arranged his
columns in an elongated octagon supporting archi-
trave, frieze and cornice, and on this placed his
dome, which he pierced with four oval windows
enriched within. The aisles were flat with entablatures radiating from the pillars to the walls and
across the north-east and south-east corners.

GALLERIES
The larger accommodation required after the Great
Fire made necessary an increased use of galleries,
and a lot has been written to show that Wren dis-
liked them and never really solved the difficult

68   St Mildred, Bread Street, *c*.1926

69   The vestry, St Lawrence Jewry, *c*.1937

problem of introducing satisfactorily a great mass of carpentry midway up his supports and rising outwards towards the aisle walls.

At St Bride he added little pilasters each side of the double columns to give visible support, but at St Andrew, Holborn [62] and St Clement Danes, he in a more logical manner placed his columns on panelled piers and interposed his gallery between. At Christ Church the pillars, and at St Andrew-by-the-Wardrobe the upper piers, were brought down directly on to the lower piers, the gallery fronts being stopped each side, perhaps not quite so satisfactory a method. All these were destroyed in the Second World War, but except for Christ Church, have now been rebuilt.

Wren's Gothic Interiors:

St Alban's had a widely spaced arcade of very depressed arches and a north projection or transept but the apse was added by Scott (1858).

St Mary Aldermary is remarkable for its oblique east wall and for its elaborate plaster fan vaulting [144]. In the spandrels of the arcades are renaissance cartouches of the Arms of Rogers (by whose gift the church was rebuilt) and of the archbishop of Canterbury, St Mary's being one of his 'peculiars'.[1]

---

[1] 13 churches in the City of London were in the diocese of Canterbury and not that of London. They were known as the archbishop of Canterbury's peculiars (of which Bow Church was the chief) and were abolished in 1841 (or 1845?).

FOUR

The Churches of Sir Christopher Wren: Furniture and Fittings

FITTINGS

While Wren had to build his churches out of public funds, the furniture was mostly supplied by the parishes and occasional private benefactions (but see page 32).

Besides the universal pewing, the following fittings were considered necessary or desirable in a City church at the close of the seventeenth century:

Carved communion table, generally of wood, with a set of silver or silver-gilt communion plate.

Elaborate carved reredos with the Creed, the Ten Commandments and the Lord's Prayer, often with paintings or effigies of Moses and Aaron.

Altar-rails, usually of wood, turned and carved, but sometimes of wrought iron, and, in one case, of brass (All Hallows, Barking).

Splendidly carved hexagonal pulpit with parquetry panels and sounding board[1] of imposing size.

A marble baluster font, with carved wooden cover, sometimes adorned with statuettes and surmounted by a dove.

A fine 'branch' (chandelier) depending from the ceiling.

A sword rest for the Lord Mayor, when he visited the church in state.[2] It was nearly always of decorative ironwork, and usually bore the Royal Arms, the City Arms, and those of the chief magistrate.

A staff for the beadle, the head, generally of silver, bearing a statue of the patron saint or other emblem.

Special enriched pews for the churchwardens, and galleries on one, two or three sides of the church, that at the west end bearing the organ (where such a luxury could be afforded),[3] usually by Father Bernard Schmidt or Renatus Harris, in a finely carved case.

A coloured plaster panel, framed painting, or, more commonly, a woodcarving of the Royal Arms, heraldic witness to the King's supremacy.

Fine inner doorcases and perhaps some bread-shelves for the dole-giving, with a framed list of benefactions – also a poor-box and fire-fighting appliances. And, of course, the bells, varying from a single bell to a whole peal; while, as the years went by, there would accumulate on the walls and pillars those often extravagantly worded, but elegant, memorial tablets, adorned with 'boys',

---

[1] Called in the accounts the 'type', as is also the font-cover.

[2] E. H. Freshfield says in Arch. 54, p. 41, that until the middle of last century it was customary for the Lord Mayor to attend in state one or other of the City churches every Sunday.

[3] In Hatton, 1708, only twelve of Wren's newly-finished churches are described as having organs, but several others are known to have had them.

70   Part of the altar-rails, St Mary Woolnoth

71   St Michael Royal: figure of Charity from organ gallery in All Hallows-the-Great (now part of a lectern)

cherubs' heads, armorial bearings and emblems of mortality.[1]

The Vestry Minutes and Churchwardens Accounts give the names and details as to the work of many of the craftsmen responsible for producing this great mass of furniture and fittings. And it is remarkable that so far as is known, for the parish records are far from complete, Grinling Gibbons is mentioned but twice – in connection with St Mary Abchurch, where he received £100 (at least) for carving the splendid altarpiece[2] and All Hallows, Barking where the famous font cover is his work (Churchwardens Accounts, 1682).

But most of the fine carving in the City churches – so repeatedly put down as Gibbons' work – is in reality very unlike it, being perhaps more honest as craftsmanship in wood than the amazing examples of virtuosity for which he is famed.

The chief among the craftsmen employed by the vestries were the following (most of these worked also for Wren at St Paul's and on the churches):

Masons
Thomas and Edward Strong, Christopher Kempster, J. Marshall, Thomas Cartwright and Edward Pearce (also a carver); the Strongs, Kempster, Marshall and Cartwright being his right-hand men.
Carpenters
Matthew Banks and John Longland.
Joiners
Will Cleere, Stephen College, Thomas Creecher, Roger Davies, William Grey and Richard Kedge.
Carvers
Richard Cleere, Wm. Emmett, Grinling Gibbons, Jonathan Maine, Wm. Newman and Ed. Pearce.
Plasterers
Henry Doogood and John Grove.
Painters
Ed. Bird, Wm. Davies, Robert Streeter, Richard Newman and Wm. Thompson.
Bell-founders
J. Bartlett and J. Hodson.
Clocks
John Wise.

The Parish Books also have interesting entries showing the supervision of Sir Christopher Wren over the work. The parishes seem to have made their own choice of tradesmen – often by competition as at St Stephen Walbrook; there were 'offers' for the altarpiece and pulpit and several for an outside clock. The first of these items, by Creecher, was with modifications actually carried out.

At St Michael, Wood Street, in 1673, the churchwardens got Wren to go with them to 'a church in Lumber Street' to see the arrangements there[3] – compare the similar inspection for St Stephen Walbrook described on p. 36.

Taking St Stephen's again as a sample, the following entries are of interest:

4th April 1679 A Convenient Font to be made by Mr. Thomas Strong.

Mr. William Davis to do all . . . painting work on the exterior.

Ed. Bird, painter, was paid for work about the vane of Walbrook, Ap. 1687:

for 22 ft of Gilding the Cinq-foyle at iiiis £4. 8. 0
for strowing (strewing) the Vane Iron
  with blue   £0. 14. 0
_____
(These two items from Building Accounts) £5. 2. 0

Here are some selections from the individual craftsmen's bills (Guildhall Library):

MASON'S WORK
Mr Strong, Jan. 2, 1677–8 A Bill for makeing of the Brick Arches for the pews for Wallbrook Church –

ffor 1000 of bricks att 15s. pr thousand	15	0
ffor 100 of lime at 10s. pr hundred	10	0
ffor 6 days worke of a mason	15	0
ffor 6 days worke of a labourer	10	0
	£2 10	0
ffor my Proffitt	5	0
	£2 15	0

[1] It is curious but there is nothing essentially Christian about these charming designs.
[2] This was discovered in 1946 in a chest belonging to the parish of St Lawrence Pountney (united with St Mary's) where accounts recorded payments to Gibbons and two letters from him were found.
[3] Either St Edmund or St Mary Woolnoth; for All Hallows, the third Lombard Street church, was not commenced till 1686.

JOINER'S WORK

John Longland got £85 10s. 0d. for preparing the flooring for the bottoms of the pews and for plates, braces and posts for the pulpit.

Roger Davies and Stephen College for pewing the church and apparently lining the walls as well received about £200 each.

CARVING

Jonathan Maine. For carving on the pews and round a doorcase, received £52 6s. 4d. and £10 extra for as many palms with Arms of the Grocers' Company on the wainscotting.

'Mr Thos. Creecher' got £75 5s. 0d. 'for the Pulpit and tipe made Readey and finished up.'

'Mr William Newman' was paid £16 9s. 11d. and £23 12s. 0½d. for carving the same.

Here are some individual items:

Body of Pulpit

ffor 14 ffot of Rafel[1] leave Beeds and Leaves at 2s. 4d. per fft	1	12	8
ffor 30 ffot 9 ynches of Leaves and fflowers Round ye Panells at 3s. per fft	4	12	3
ffor 5 peices of ffouldige and Books at 12s. pce.	3	0	0
ffor 6 Corner peices of ffouldige at 10s. pce.	3	0	0

About ye Type

ffor 6 Boys and ffestoones at 30s. each	9	0	0
ffor 30 ffoot of large Rafel leaves at 1s. per ff.	1	10	0
ffor 16 ffoot 8 ynches of hollow and huske at 1s. per fft.		16	8
ffor 6 Cheribims heads at 6s. per pce.	1	16	0
ffor the Ionick Capitall	2	0	0

Newman received for the altarpiece £41 3s. 3d., of which £8 10s. 0d. went on the King's Arms and for the rail and banister £10 17s. 0d. The 51 banisters cost 2s. each. For carving the communion table he got £6.

As directed by the Vestry, Thomas Strong made the font, for which he got £45 paid for by instalments.

The joiner, whose name is not given, received:

ffor a Tipe made ready for the funt and delivered without the carving	12	0	0

Here is Newman's bill in full (no date):

ffor the Carving the type of the fount –

ffor all the mouldins	1	15	0
ffor 8 Capitelles 3s. apeece	1	4	0
ffor 8 flouer potes 3s. 6d. apeece	1	8	0
ffor 8 festones and chiribines heades and notes 6s. apeece	2	8	0
ffor 8 peeces of fouldig and bayes 6s. apeece	2	8	0
ffor 8 figures 15s. apeece	6	0	0
ffor 1 Croune		10	0
	£15	13	0

PAINTING

Mr. Wm. Davies, Painter's Bill, 2 July 1679:

Imprimis ffor 2200 of gold roses . . . at 16s. per hundred	17	12	0
Layd out for the over glase		2	6
ffor writing of the Commandments, the Lord's Prayer and Creed	5	0	0
ffor painting of the pulpit irons, the over glass iron and Sord Case		15	0
ffor painting of Moses and Aaron and the King's Armes	5	0	0
ffor painting the iron work of the pews and numbering of ye same	1	10	0
	£29	19	6

A good idea of what Wren's churches looked like when fresh from the workmen's hands can be gathered from Hatton's *New View of London*, 1708, which gives an obviously authoritative description of each church and its fittings of which the following is an example:

St Edmund the King situated on the North-side of Lombard Street in Langbourn Ward was rebuilt of Stone in 1690 and of the Tuscan Order. Built so that the greatest length is from North to South and Altarpiece at North end. I believe it was done to save ground whereon to build Houses fronting the Street which here fetch very great Rents. . . . The Roof is flat, and has enrichments of Quadrangles with Crocket-work within, and Festoons, Vases &c. without.

Here is a neat little Organ Gallery, and the

---

[1] Also spelt 'raffled' or 'rapehild', an old word for acanthus foliage, to raffle being to indent or serrate (a leaf).

Church is very well pewed and wainscotted with Oak 5 Ft. high, and also 2 Doorcases of the same, with Pilasters of the Corinthian Order and Enrichments of Shields, Palm-branches &c.

The Pulpit is finely carved, the Sound-board (now gone) Conical, with Festoons, Cherubims &c.

The Font is near the South-West Corner of the Church, of Marble, and the Type is wainscot well carved, having the figures of the Twelve Apostles[1] in a standing posture in two ranges round it and enrichments of Cherubims &c.

The Altar Piece is pretty spacious. . . . On the West side of the Church is the Queen's Arms and against them on the East side is a painted Monument like a Hatchment (with her Arms and Supporters), in memory of Queen Mary with the words below, "In Memoria Augustiss & Exopatatiss Reginæ Mariæ morte præmatura, Dec. 28 1694 Cœlo redditæ".

Here also are pertinent Texts of Scripture painted on carved Boards and placed round the Church about the space, of 8 Ft. from each other. Prayers at 11 and 7 Daily. 147 Houses.

One is tempted to think what a wonderful place London two years later must have been with the newly finished cathedral and 50 churches raising their unsullied Portland stone and lead over streets of comely red brick houses; but alas for this high-flown fantasy! – the noted German traveller, Zacharias Conrad von Uffenbach, on a visit to London in 1710, says in his diary, after an enthusiastic description of St Paul's, 'One must yet lament that it stands here, for it is already so black with coal-smoke that it has lost half its elegance'![2]

Still, in spite of this, to wander into any of these half a hundred churches and find them completely fitted out with beautiful examples (in mint condition) of a healthy traditional yet modern art must have been a thrill.

The only interior – and what a beautiful one! – still retaining all its original furniture was at St Mildred, Bread Street, and that, alas, has been completely destroyed. And except for unsuitable stained glass windows and ugly electric light standards before the reredos, there were no modern intrusions. Other interiors notable for their fittings

were at St Mary Magdelen (burnt 1886, demolished *c*.1890), All Hallows-the-Great (demolished 1894), All Hallows, Lombard Street (demolished 1939), St Lawrence Jewry, St Magnus and St Mary Abchurch, while less known examples were at St Clement Eastcheap, St Martin, Ludgate, St Stephen, Coleman Street, and elsewhere.

Unfortunately the low esteem in which these fine works of Sir Christopher and his craftsmen were held in the nineteenth century led not only to the deliberate destruction of many of the churches, but also to a craze for rearranging the interiors. Consequent on a demand for a 'chancel', the choir was in every case (except St Mildred, Bread Street) brought down from the west gallery and provided with stalls close to the altar; often the organ also was brought down and placed on the floor near the choir. The pews, necessities in the old days of unheated churches, were cut down, or – much worse – removed altogether and replaced by open benches, often of poor design.

The panels of the reredos were frequently painted out and pictures of saints substituted, or their places covered by large religious paintings. And, last but not least, the beautiful clear-glazed windows of many panes were filled with indifferent stained glass, often so dark as to necessitate artificial light on the brightest day. Or an even worse fate might befall them as at St Mary Aldermanbury, St Michael, Cornhill and St Swithun where mullions and tracery of Italianesque design were inserted first.

The following is a typical, though rather extreme example of this Victorian vandalism. Dr Philip Norman describing St Michael, Wood Street in 1897 says:

'The pulpit . . . has lost its sounding board and its old stair balustrade has been replaced by a modern one. . . . The high pews disappeared in 1888 being replaced by yellow deal benches and chancel stalls with ends of pseudo-Gothic design; gas standards brazen to match were also provided. The organ . . . was brought down from

---

[1] Only four of these now remain.
[2] *London in 1710*, Faber & Faber, 1934, p. 35.

the western gallery and placed on the floor at the north west corner, that same gallery being mutilated . . . to make room for it. The organ-case has gone, and the pipes have been stencilled over with a diaper pattern utterly inappropriate. The marble font . . . with its carved . . . cover . . . has been daubed over with paint and is now in the south west corner'.

But in spite of all this wrongheadedness and misguided zeal a large quantity of really fine work remained up to 1940; of this, with other examples formerly existing, the following items were the most remarkable.

ALTAR-PIECE OR REREDOS:
The only pre-Fire reredos in the City known to the writer was, prior to 1828, in St Bartholomew-the-Great [7]; it is pictured in Wilkinson's *Londina Illustrata* c.1825 and is described in a parish document of 1821 as 'an altar piece 32 feet high consisting of a very spacious piece of architecture painted on canvas' with the usual inscriptions. On the upper part are the arms of King Charles I with the initials 'C.R.' They were later altered to G.R. There was a Glory above the Commandments but the most prominent feature of the whole design was the Royal Arms which were enormous. The table itself was insignificant.

Though always having to include the Decalogue, etc., with or without Moses and Aaron and a Glory or other emblem of the Deity, frequently with the Royal Arms in the above unseemly position, the altar-pieces of Wren's churches show an astonishing variety of design from the long low reredos at

72 St Margaret Lothbury, *c.* 1885

73 Reredos, St Martin, Ludgate

74   Reredos by Grinling Gibbons, St Mary Abchurch

St Stephen, Coleman Street, to the lofty erection formerly at Bow church.[1]

Among the finest reredoses (besides these two) are, or were, those at St Mildred, Bread Street, St Augustine, St Bartholomew-by-the-Exchange (latterly in St Giles Cripplegate), St Martin, Ludgate, St Magnus, St Mary Abchurch,[2] St Vedast (the four latter superb and unspoilt until 1940), and the truly magnificent example at All Hallows, Lombard Street (removed in 1939 to Twickenham,[3] while at St Bride formerly existed what must have been one of the most sumptuous altar-pieces in London. The altar-piece at St Clement Eastcheap, after Victorian tampering, was restored and gorgeously decorated by J. N. Comper. At St Mary Woolnoth, by Hawksmoor, is a splendid reredos of about 1720.

Here are Hatton's descriptions of the pieces at Bow church and at St Bride:

St Mary-le-Bow:
The Altar-piece is Oak, very neat, newly erected and painted. It is adorned (below) with 4 fluted Pilasters and Entablature of the Corinthian Order, 2 on each side of the Decalogue, done in gold Letters on Black under a Glory all in one square Frame carved and gilt, and above are 2 Attick Pilasters with Cornish and Compass

---

[1] This was actually cut in two, the upper part being removed to show the miserable stained glass then inserted in the east window (and throughout the church) about 1870 or 1880.
[2] Gibbons.
[3] See note 2 on p. 79.

75 Reredos, St Vedast

Pediment, whereon are placed the Figures of 7 golden Candlesticks with flaming Tapers. Under this Pediment in a spacious Glory, the Rays curiously Finnier'd, replenishing a Circle about 5 Foot Diameter; in the centre the Words 'Glory be to God on high', and under in one line without the Circle, 'In Earth Peace, Goodwill towards men'. This upper part of the Altar-piece is enriched with Palm-branches, Leaves and Voluta's, between 2 Lamps; and all the before-mentioned placed between 2 spacious beautiful Columns,[1] painted in imitation of Lapis Lazuli; and their Entablature is painted like Porphyry, the Capitals and Enrichments hereof being gilt with Gold; and without these Columns are placed the Lord's Prayer and Creed.[2]

St Bride:

The Altar-piece beautiful and magnificent. The lower part consists of 6 carved Columns (painted Flake-stone colour) with Entablature and circular Pediments of the Corinthian Order, embellis'd with Lamps, Cherubims, etc., all gilt with gold. Above a circular Pediment are the Queen's Arms, finely carved, gilt, and painted with the Supporters. Under the Pediment a Text, 1 Cor. c. 10, v. 16. Inter-columns, the Decalogue, Paternoster and Creed.

The upper Part is painted, and consists of 6 Columns (3 on each side of a handsome arched 5 Light Window, adorned with a neat Scarletsilk Curtain, edged with Gold Fringe) with their Entablature finely done (white and veined) in strong Perspective. In front of which are the Pourtraictures of Moses, with the Two Tables in his Hands, and Aaron in his Priest's Habit; over the Window 'tis painted Nebulous, and above the Clouds appears (from within a large Crimson Velvet Festoon painted Curtain) a Celestial Choir, or a Representation of the Church Triumphant, in the Vision and Presence of a Glory in the shape of a Dove, all finely painted, the Enrichments are gilt with Gold.

At the Spanish and Portuguese synagogue, Bevis Marks, there is a splendid altar-piece (in everything but name), the Echal, or cupboard for enclosing the ark being a beautiful piece of furniture with Corinthian pillars, scrolls, vases, etc., and similar to the finest reredoses mentioned about. It dates from about 1703.

Of later reredoses the finest is at St Mary Woolnoth. Very distinctive, it consists of a lofty canopy supported by massive twisted columns (all gold and black) enclosing under a richly carved and gilt choir of angels two panels of the Decalogue beautifully written with flourishes in gold on red, now covered by new lettering.

COMMUNION TABLES AND RAILS

At St Stephen Walbrook is a fine but very small table of semi-elliptical form with beautifully carved rails of the same shape. Other fine examples occurred at St Mary Abchurch, All Hallows, Barking, St Mildred, Bread Street, St Stephen, Coleman Street [76], and St Benet, Paul's Wharf [77], the latter two with figure supports. The table in All Hallows-the-Great was of unique design – a marble slab upheld by a kneeling figure of an angel. It was removed in 1856 and later lost. St Katherine Cree has an Adam or Hepplewhite table.

The finest carved wooden rails were at St Olave, Hart Street (with four little projecting couchant lions), St Stephen, Coleman Street, St Stephen Walbrook, and elsewhere. All Hallows, Barking had rails of brass with turned balusters; St Magnus and St Mary Woolnoth [70] have wrought iron examples.

CHURCH PLATE

The City churches possess a vast quantity of plate, including many pieces of unusual interest and beauty, but it is too great a subject to be dealt with here. Those interested should consult the volume by Edwin Freshfield (privately printed) on the Church Plate of the City of London. The large flagons at St Mary Woolnoth, beautifully chased, are the finest of their kind in the City. They date from 1587.[3]

---

[1] Ranging with those all round the church.

[2] In front of the two side windows.

[3] One of them, under the last rector, crossed the Atlantic on, I believe, permanent loan to a church in Victoria, British Columbia.

76 Communion table, St Stephen, Coleman Street

77 Communion table, St Benet, Paul's Wharf

PULPITS

At St Bartholomew-the-Great the mediaeval pulpit, five-sided with traceried panels, survived until 1828.[1] At All Hallows, Barking [13] and St Helen [14] were two very fine Jacobean examples with sounding-boards, the latter surviving. Of those of the Wren period many have lost their 'types' and some have been removed to the suburbs.

As we know from the foregoing extracts, one parish often took another's furniture as a pattern for its own, with the result that designs were duplicated, though of course with varied details. The following examples with sounding-boards were remaining up to 1940. The makers' names when ascertainable are given.

1. *Pairs*

St Mary Abchurch (Grey, joiner; Emmett or Newman, carver) and All Hallows, Lombard Street (Grey and Mitchell, joiners). Only the types correspond; the pulpits differ.

St Clement Eastcheap and All Hallows-the-Great, now at St Paul's, Hammersmith. Lovely pulpits with oval panels; Cupids with swags on the types.

---

[1] Described and pictured in Webb's *Records of St Bartholomew's, Smithfield*, 1921.

78   St Mary Abchurch

79   St Clement Eastcheap before Butterfield's alterations of 1872

St Magnus (Grey, joiner) and St Lawrence Jewry [80] (Kedge, joiner; Pearce, carver). Pulpits with semi-oval panels above square ones; urns and swags on the types.

St Stephen Walbrook (Creecher, joiner; Newman, carver) is of similar design, but with cupids instead of urns on the type, which formerly had an ogee dome.

St Peter, Cornhill and St Augustine, now – largely renewed – at St Anne and St Agnes, with arched panels on the pulpit.

80   St Lawrence Jewry

81   St Stephen Walbrook

82   St Augustine, Watling Street

2. *Single examples*

St Mildred, Bread Street – superb, now destroyed

St Dionis Backchurch – now at Fulham

St James Garlickhithe – from St Michael Queenhithe

St Vedast – now destroyed

The last three have types with enriched but not shaped edges. St Vedast's type must have been renewed or altered as it differs from Hatton's description: 'On the Sound-Board the Figures of seven gilded Candlesticks with Wax Tapers and as many Stars of 8 Rays.'

Among the finest pulpits without types are, or were, those at St Andrew Undershaft [84] with

83   Pulpit, St Mildred, Bread Street

84   St Andrew Undershaft

85 Pulpit, St Swithun, now in All Hallows, Barking

circular panels, St Swithun[1] [85] with curved pediments, St Stephen, Coleman Street, St Andrew, Holborn, St Edmund, and Christ Church [88], which formerly possessed two examples. One of these it obtained from the Temple church in 1840, and the other, the original, was unique in having figure subjects – carvings of the Last Supper and the four evangelists. Latterly it was broken up and the panels incorporated in the choir stalls – now destroyed.

The pulpit at St Clement Danes, with inlaid circular panels amid much foliage, is very elaborate but like much of the plasterwork in the church its

---

[1] The type was sold as old timber in 1860!

86   St Stephen, Coleman Street

87   St Edmund, Lombard Street

88   Christ Church, Newgate Street:
pulpit from Temple church

decoration is rather overdone. Of later pulpits, St Mary Woolnoth possesses a square example with type; finely carved, but of rather inelegant outline. At St Botolph, Aldgate the pulpit dates from about 1745, very simple except for remarkable inlaid devices. At All Hallows-on-the-Wall, still later, the plain pulpit is built into the wall and only entered from the vestry.

HOUR-GLASSES

Very few have survived but at St Alban, Wood Street there was a fine specimen on a twisted stand fixed to the pulpit, the frame of bronze embossed with cherubs' heads and angels blowing trumpets and crested with crosses and fleur de lys [89].

89 Hour-glass from St Alban, Wood Street (now at St Vedast)

90 Font, St Lawrence Jewry

FONTS

The only mediaeval font is the plain fifteenth-century one at St Bartholomew-the-Great, but there are three later pre-Fire examples in the City: St Helen, *c.*1632, St Andrew Undershaft, *c.*1634 by Nicholas Stone and St Katherine Cree, *c.*1633, the gift of Sir John Gayer (in whose memory the 'Lion Sermon' is annually preached), while another similar to the last was formerly in St Ethelburga.

91   Font, All Hallows, Lombard Street (now at Twickenham)

92   All Hallows-by-the-Tower, showing Grinling Gibbons' font cover

93   Christ Church, Newgate Street, showing font

94   Font, St Stephen Walbrook   95   Font, St Magnus   96   Font cover,
St Botolph, Aldgate

The fonts of the Wren period usually consisted of a vase-like bowl and baluster stem. The font at St Margaret, Lothbury has figure subjects carved on the bowl: the Fall of Man, Noah's Ark, the Baptism of Christ, and that of the Eunuch. The type at All Hallows, Barking [92], by Gibbons is *sui generis*, being a flat circular tray with thereon three Cupids supporting a sort of sheaf of festoons of fruit and flowers, topped with a dove; Malcolm says they are stealing the grapes! The font itself was of grey-blue marble.

Though the bowls and balusters show great variety of shape and decoration,[1] the types are still more varied and range from fluted or ribbed tureen-like covers often resembling a crown (St Margaret Pattens, St James Garlickhithe, St Nicholas Cole Abbey, etc.), to elaborate, shaped canopies with figures etc. (Christ Church, St Edmund, St Stephen Walbrook [94]), or architectural designs as at St Mary Abchurch, St Magnus [95], and St Giles Cripplegate.

At St Clement Eastcheap, St Margaret, Lothbury,

[1] In two cases (St Magnus and St Bartholomew-by-the-Exchange) the support was cruciform in section, being four consoles – scrolled pilasters – back to back.

and St Peter, Cornhill are types consisting of a series of shaped scrolls, topped with cherubs' heads uniting to uphold a flaming urn and enclosing a Holy Dove. The font at St Vedast was oval in shape.

ORGANS

As pointed out before, this now universal instrument of church music was in Wren's time more often conspicuous by its absence. In *New Remarks of London*, 1732 (compiled by the various parish clerks) out of the 53 Wren churches, 20 only are stated to have had organs, 27 to be without them

97   Organ, St James Garlickhithe

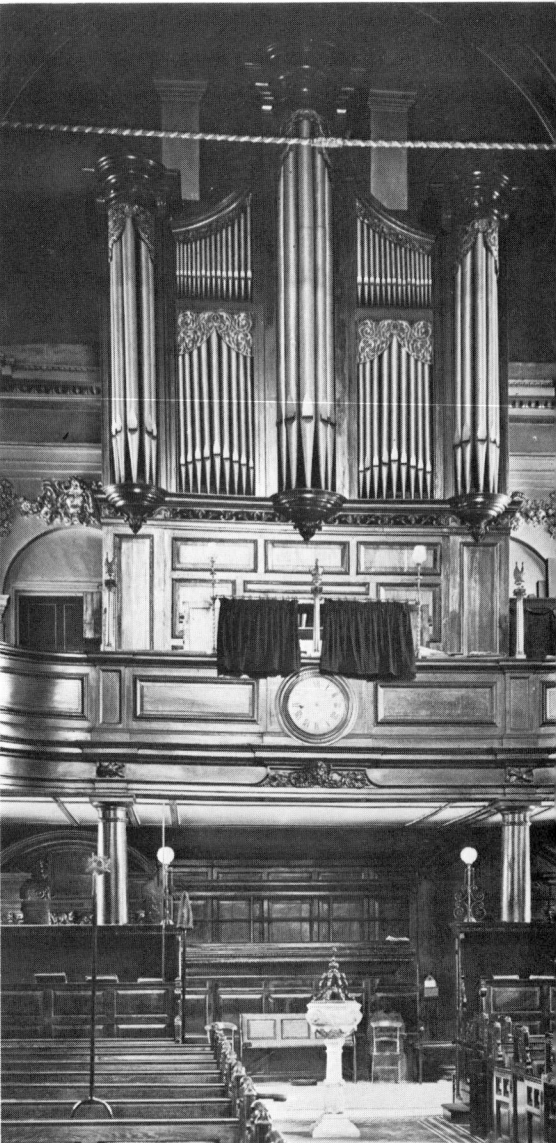

98   St Peter, Cornhill: west end organ

(including St Mary-le-Bow and St Stephen Walbrook!), and at six others the organ is not mentioned. But St Clement Danes and St Sepulchre, included in these six, are known to have had fine instruments, which makes 22 to 27 and four indeterminate. St Stephen Walbrook had no organ till 1765, and St Mary Aldermary till 1781! Eventually all the City churches had organs except St

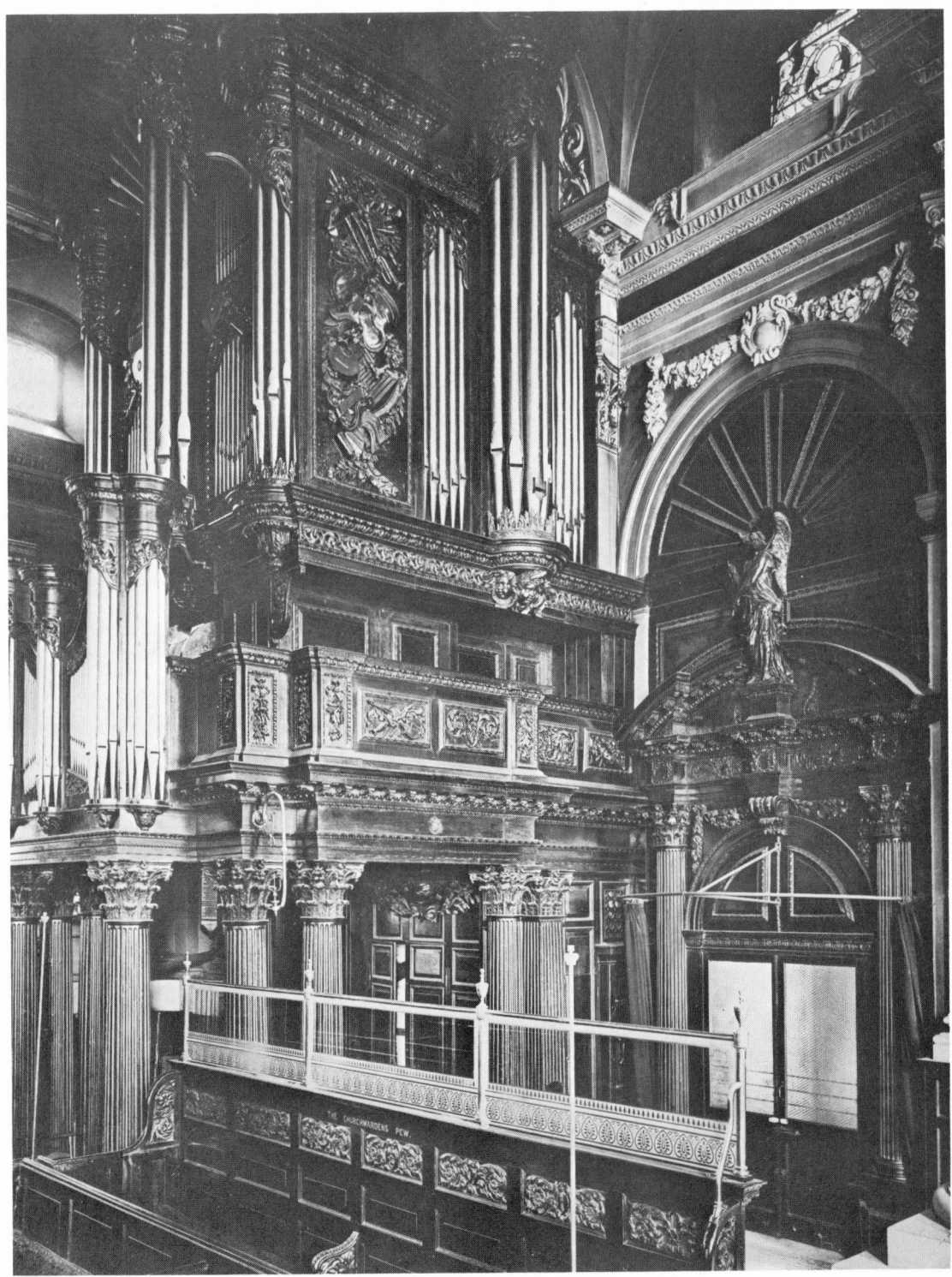

99   Organ, St Lawrence Jewry, from Birch's *London Churches*, 1896

Benet Gracechurch and St Christopher-le-Stocks.

The organ in a handsome case was always placed on a west gallery or loft. They were nearly all built by Smith or Harris, of whose rivalry unpleasant tales are told. Their organs (up to 1711) were divided between them thus:

Harris (1670–1711) Christ Church, All Hallows, Barking, All Hallows, Lombard Street, St Andrew, Holborn, St Andrew Undershaft, St Botolph, Aldgate, St Bride, St Clement Eastcheap, St Giles Cripplegate, St Lawrence Jewry [99], St Michael, Cornhill, St Sepulchre.

Smith (1681–1708) (Besides St Paul's and the Temple church) St Dunstan-in-the-East, St James Garlickhithe [97], St Katherine Cree, St Martin,

100   St Stephen Walbrook: Rococo organ case of 1765 on 17th-century west screen

Ludgate, St Mary-at-Hill, St Mary Woolnoth, St Peter, Cornhill [98], St Clement Danes, St Peter-ad-Vincula, Tower of London.

Abraham Jordan built the fine instrument at St Magnus in 1712, which contains the first example of a 'swell-organ'. He also built the little organ at St Benet Fink, 1714.

The most magnificent case was at St Lawrence Jewry, supported on Corinthian pillars and flanked by two equally handsome doorways, forming a composition unrivalled for richness and beauty. Other splendid examples are at All Hallows, Lombard Street, St Andrew Undershaft, St James Garlickhithe, St Magnus and St Peter-ad-Vincula. The late organ case at St Stephen Walbrook [100], though of the rococo period, is so designed as to harmonize with the Wren fittings in a remarkable way. At St Mary Aldermary the 1781 organ had a charming 'Gothick' case with attenuated finials on the turrets; it was removed in 1876 [132].

SCREENS

In two cases a carved screen spanned the church – at St Peter, Cornhill (a Wren design), and at All Hallows-the-Great, the gift of Theodore Jacobsen, one of the merchants of the Steelyard, situate in the parish, who are commemorated by a carved eagle of the Hanseatic towns in the centre – and on the sounding-board of the pulpit which he also gave. This beautiful screen was removed to St Margaret, Lothbury in 1894.

SWORD RESTS

It appears that sword cases, as they were called, did not come into general use until after the Restoration, and very few examples survive of an earlier date than the end of Queen Anne's reign. While some churches are without rests, others have more than one, and this is occasioned in part by the union of parishes but more often because successive aldermen often presented new ones upon being elevated to the Chair.

At first they were of wood, and specimens remain at St Helen, 1665 [101], St Mary Aldermary, 1682 [102], Southwark cathedral (from St Olave, Tooley Street), 1674, and two in Companies' Halls. The first of these is of unique design, consisting of two wreathed columns with entablature bearing the

101   St Helen, Bishopsgate: wooden sword-rest of 1665

102   Wooden sword-rest of 1682, St Mary Aldermary

103   Sword-rests, All Hallows-by-the-Tower, from Birch's *London Churches*, 1896

Arms of the City, with, above, the Royal Arms supported by angels, and those of Sir John Lawrence, the heroic Lord Mayor of the Plague Year. The rest at St Mary, by far the finest of the other four, is of quite different design, elaborate with carved flowers, drapery, etc., and the Royal Arms, supported by flying cherubs.

The later sword rests were of iron, and are of two kinds – those having a central pole and those without that feature. The earliest dated example is at St Magnus, 1708.[1] In St Dunstan-in-the-East were a pair of brass rests, made for the rebuilt church; at St Mary-at-Hill is a fine series.

BEADLES' STAVES

These, originally their symbols of office though now carried by churchwardens in processions, are of three kinds: first, those with plain pear-shaped knobs; second, those with statuettes, models or other devices; and third, short maces or wands.

104 Beadle's silver badge, St Giles Cripplegate

Those extant date from 1677 to 1861, and are all described and many illustrated in Freshfield's book on the London church plate, mentioned on p. 86.

GALLERIES

The fronts of these were usually panelled in a plain manner, but those formerly at St Sepulchre were richly carved, and the handsome fronts at St Bride were of very unusual design. Until 1871 St Clement Eastcheap had a delicately detailed gallery, while the beautiful fronts of those formerly in St Mary Woolnoth are preserved against the walls.

CHURCHWARDENS' PEWS

The finest are at St Margaret Pattens, where they are canopied, as were also those of St Bartholomew-by-the-Exchange.

KING'S BEASTS

The lion and unicorn holding shields were placed on the front pews at many churches to mark the division between nave and chancel.

ROYAL ARMS

The finest examples in plaster were at Christ Church, St Michael Bassishaw (between two cartouches of the City Arms, removed about 1900 to the Guildhall Museum), and St Mildred, Bread Street. Carved wooden examples are very numerous, as at St Margaret Pattens, All Hallows, Lombard Street (now at Twickenham), etc. The Arms of William III can be distinguished from those of the Stuarts by a small shield of Orange-Nassau. The Royal Arms underwent three distinct changes in the early eighteenth century and a fourth in 1800–01.

DOORCASES

St Helen has two beautiful examples of c.1633; while, of the Wren period, at St Martin, Ludgate [66], and St Mary Abchurch [58], there is a fine series, and other good examples occurred at St Lawrence Jewry [101], St Nicholas Cole Abbey and All Hallows, Lombard Street [66]. One of these at the latter church until 1865 formed the entrance from the street, and is covered with carvings of bones, skulls and hour-glasses [133].

[1] Those interested should consult E.H. Freshfield's article in *Archaeologia* 45, p. 41.

105   Plasterwork in gallery, St Andrew, Holborn

STAINED AND PAINTED GLASS

Little coloured glass had survived 1666, and little at all notable has been made for the City since. Of the earlier glass, St Andrew Undershaft retains the largest amount. The heads of the aisle windows contain the arms of contributors to the rebuilding of 1532 (originally 44 in all, see Guide), and the west window is filled with a fine composition (formerly in the east window) containing the portraits of Edward VI, Elizabeth, James I, Charles I and Charles II or William III, with, below, the Stuart Royal Arms (with supporters holding flags) between those of the Tudors and William III. It is said to be of late seventeenth-century date, but apart from the fact that in old engravings the figures do not correspond and the background, etc., is quite different, it is nothing like work of that period but closely resembles Powell's heraldic work under Pugin at the Houses of Parliament. Is it a nineteenth-century window on the old lines? There is a little pre-Fire glass at St Helen, St Ethelburga and St Katherine Cree.

The only surviving glass of the Wren period was in St Andrew, Holborn [106 and 108] and St Edmund. In the first was a window of the Arms of Queen Anne, before the Union with Scotland, and at St Edmund was another, 'Set up in the memorable year of Union, 1707' [107]. Corresponding with the Queen's Arms on the north at St Andrew were those of Thavies Inn on the south, a beautiful window, and between them the great east window of six lights was filled with magnificent glass signed 'Joshua Price, 1718'. The subject of the three lower lights was the Last Supper, while those above depicted the Ascension. All this early eighteenth-century glass is now destroyed.

St Giles Cripplegate had a delightful elliptical east window (1791) with cherubs round a Glory, and the early 'Gothick' glass at St Dunstan-in-the-East is mentioned on p. 113. At St Dunstan, Fleet Street was a finely designed but rather brilliant window by Willement, Herald-Painter to George IV, designer of the glass in the Great Hall at Hampton Court. He also executed the east window at St Stephen Walbrook, 1850. These have also gone.

Of modern glass in the City mention can be made of the following:

106   St Andrew, Holborn: south-east window of *c.*1682, with arms of John Thavies

Leonard Walker – Four windows in St Ethelburga (pre-war)

Hugh Easton – All windows in St Bartholomew-the-Less, 1951

A.E. Buss – East windows, St Olave, Hart Street, 1953

107   St Edmund, Lombard Street: window of 1707 with arms of Queen Anne

108 St Andrew, Holborn: east window by Joshua
Price, 1718

Christopher Webb – All windows, St Lawrence
Jewry, 1950s
Farrer Bell & Sons – All windows (heraldic), All
Hallows, Barking, 1948–58
John Hayward – All windows, St Mary-le-Bow,
1964
    Four windows, St Michael Royal, 1968
    Window over south porch, St Olave, Hart
    Street (good heraldry)
Keith New – East window, St Stephen Walbrook,
1961

East windows, St Nicholas Cole Abbey, 1962
Brian Thomas – East windows and one in west
chapel, St Andrew, Holborn, *c.*1960
East windows, St Vedast, 1961
St Andrew-by-the-Wardrobe – south aisle, four
windows by Carl Edwards
The following churches have glass by several
contemporary artists:
    St Mary Aldermary – East and south-east
    window, Lawrence Lee
    West window, John Crawford
    St Sepulchre – Musicians chapel, two windows
        by Brian Thomas
    East window, G.E.R. Smith, 1949
    South aisle, Capt John Smith, Francis Skeat,
        1968
    St Magnus – South aisle, Lawrence Lee, 1950–52
    North aisle (circular, heraldic), Alfred
    Wilkinson, 1953–60
    Austin Friars (opened 1954) – Great west win-
        dow, Max Nanta
    East window, Hugh Easton
    North side (good, heraldic) small panel,
    William Wilson, 1954–58

PAINTING
There appears to be no mediaeval painted decoration remaining in the City churches but some survived from the Wren period. Besides the numerous
paintings of Moses and Aaron, and St Bride's
wonderful reredos, St Olave Jewry originally had
three curious examples. Hatton says:

In this church as a farther Ornament, here are
three spacious Pieces of Painting viz:
1. That on the North Side of the Chancel is
Queen Elizabeth lying on a fine Tomb adorned
with Columns, of the Corinthian Order with the
Regalia and under an Arched Canopy on which
is placed her Arms between 2 Cupids; but no
inscription.
2. The Picture of King Charles the First (which
was allegorical).
3. At the West end . . . a very spacious and
curious Piece of Painting, in a strong black
Frame, being the Figure of Time with Wings
displaced, a Scythe in his right and an Hour-glass
in his left hand. At his right Foot is a Cupid

dormant, its head resting on lovely Fruit and another near his left Arm. Under the Feet of Time lyeth the Pourtrait of a Sceleton about 8 Foot in length, and here are depensilled the Words in Proverbs 27, 1, Job 17, 11, Deut-my 32, 29.

In the building accounts for St Mary Aldermary (in the library at St Paul's cathedral) in August 1704, William Thompson, painter, presents his bill, amounting to £10:

> for 'Painting 5 large Windows in the Church like quarries with appearance of Landskip of Trees, Sky, Cloudes etc'

These were in the blocked windows of the north aisle.

And later, about 1830, paintings on transparent blinds representing St Peter's delivery from prison and the Transfiguration had recently been hung up in the east windows of St Vedast (*Churches of London* by Godwin & Britton, 1838–39, Part II, p. 6).

The paintings in the dome of St Mary Abchurch are very extensive, the work of William Snow, painter and carver. At St Lawrence Jewry the ceiling of the vestry, representing the apotheosis of St Lawrence, 1678, and the overmantel, with his martyrdom, were by Fuller the younger, though the latter picture was also attributed to Ribera. In the north aisle was a Flemish Adoration of the Trinity, formerly the altar-piece.

At St Andrew Undershaft in 1725 Henry Tombes, 'a worthy inhabitant', paid for the church to be elaborately decorated with a 'heavenly choir' over the altar, with the 12 apostles between the clerestory windows, while in the spandrels of the arcades were monochrome paintings of the miracles of Christ. The latter series alone remain; they were black with dirt but have now been cleaned.

There are modern murals at All Hallows, Barking (Brian Thomas), St Ethelburga and St Vedast Rectory (Hans Feibusch).

VESTRIES

These were sometimes fitted up handsomely or even sumptuously, as at St Lawrence Jewry with its magnificent panelling, carving, plasterwork and painting [69]. The vestries of St Clement East-cheap and St Michael, Cornhill have handsome fireplaces, as also had St Nicholas Cole Abbey. That at St Bride was a very nice room of the Adam period, and the west vestibule was most attractive with fine doorcases and panelling.

MINOR FURNITURE

Hatstands in wrought iron occur at St James Garlickhithe, St Michael Royal, etc. There are poor-boxes in wood at St Mary Abchurch, St Peter, Cornhill, etc., and at All Hallows, Barking a fine brass one on a fluted pedestal, dated 1787, formerly at Christ's Hospital.

BRASSES AND MONUMENTS

Good examples survive at All Hallows, Barking and St Helen, and the rich store of monuments and wall tablets which abound in the City churches can only be mentioned briefly.

Of the pre-Fire churches, St Helen is richest in memorials ranging from the fourteenth to the nineteenth centuries, while at St Andrew Undershaft the many fine monuments were cleaned and the heraldry repainted about 1934. Of the Wren churches, St Dionis Backchurch was notable for its monuments and there was an imposing array on the south wall at St Vedast. Of the later churches the two St Dunstans had a fine series, in each case retaining several from the earlier church.

BELLS

St Bartholomew-the-Less has two mediaeval bells, one by John Langhorne (?), *c*.1400, and one by John Crouch, *c*.1440. St Bartholomew-the-Great has five by Thos Bullesden, *c*.1510 while All Hallows Staining had a Flemish bell of 1458 now in Grocers' Hall.

Of later bells, the founders include Robert Mot (end of sixteenth century – St Andrew Undershaft and St Stephen Walbrook), and the firm of Thomas, Anthony and James Bartlett, John Hodson, the Eldridges, Abraham Rudhall, Richard Phelps and others in the later seventeenth and early eighteenth centuries. At St Benet, Paul's Wharf, besides one in the tower by W. Wightman, 1683, is a small bell in the lantern inscribed 'Thomas Pinfold, Dr. at Laws, 1685'. Old Sanctus bells remain at St Andrew, Holborn (Robert Mot, 1587), St Edmund and St Sepulchre.

109   St Helen, Bishopsgate: effigies of Sir John Crosby and first wife, 1476

110   Memorial to Sir Nicholas Throckmorton, 1570, in
St Katherine Cree

111   St Andrew Undershaft: monument to John Stow,
1605

112 Monument to Constance Whitney, St Giles Cripple-gate

113 Mrs Pepys' monument, St Olave, Hart Street

114 Robert Preston's tombstone, 1730, in churchyard of St Magnus

FIRE EQUIPMENT

Fire-ladders (usually hung on the church walls) were used in many parishes before 1666, but were of course quite inadequate in the Great Fire. These continued to be provided but as 1666 got more and more remote people became careless and the ladders began to disappear. Many, however, remained until the nineteenth century, and old photographs show that St Mary Aldermary retained its fire-ladder until at least the 1860s.[1] Two survived until the last war at St Mary Abchurch (gone by 1947) and the penthouse supports remain. Below these were two hinged iron barriers long and short, of unknown purpose, one of which survives. If only the churches had been provided with ladders at Christmas 1940 and at subsequent raids! But hardly one remained or any other facilities for fire fighting either!

Post-Fire precautions also included buckets, 'squirts' or syringes, and engines about which latter the following extracts are of interest:

St Stephen Walbrook Churchwardens Account Books:

1708 Cash paid for new Engeons   £35.0.0
(White, *History of Walbrook Ward* 1903, p. 397). St Mildred, Poultry in an inventory of church goods 5 May 1715 contains 'Item One large Copper Engine for ffire, with 80 foot of Leather Pipe and brass screws, with a brass Socket for the Water Plug and 20 yards of Canvas Pipe and a Copper Hook to fill the Engine, and two pair of Wooden handles, and a Truck with four Wheels to draw the Engine on, And a Copper Branch to carry the Water. Also a hand Engine ('squirt'?) in the Engine House in the Churchyard with . . . bucketts'. (Milbourn's *History of the Parish*).

When parsons fail to protect the treasures committed to their charge or spoil their churches by wrong-headed 'restoration' or alterations one is justly indignant. Often fine seventeenth- and eighteenth-century fittings have been turned out of mediaeval churches or thrown aside as being incongruous. But the fact that in most cases good work of whatever period, *made for its position*, harmonizes by its very excellence with that of any other period, is not, one may venture to think, appreciated by the average churchman. But one forgets that the church is not primarily a museum, nor the incumbent the keeper of it as such. For he is not chosen for his important post on the strength of his knowledge of archaeology, architecture or art, but theoretically at least, for his ability to look after the spiritual welfare of his cure. And this is as it should be, though the result to his church (and the national heritage) is, one may admit, often deplorable. But these things are a legacy from the time when the Church was the best – almost the only – patron of the arts, and when there were no 'Ecclesiastical Furnishers' (!) for ecclesiastical and secular art were one, and this art was practised by none but craftsmen trained in a sound and living tradition.

This healthy state of things lasted until near the end of the eighteenth century, and was not finally destroyed until the Gothic revival became vitiated by the lack of taste that overcame architecture and the lesser arts in the middle of the last century, and of which the products shown at the Great Exhibition of 1851 were typical.

But things improved in the second half of the nineteenth century (in spite of the Church Furnishers) as shown by the 1971 exhibition of 'Victorian Church Art' at the Victoria and Albert Museum, and much fine work continued well into the present century. But now, with the decline of churchgoing and consequent redundancy of churches, scarcity of patronage and ever-increasing cost of materials etc, the training and maintenance of craftsmen to carry on the production of well-designed church fittings of all kinds is in serious jeopardy.

---

[1] Dickens, in *The Uncommercial Traveller* says 'Fire-ladders, which I am satisfied nobody knows anything about . . . moulder away in the larger churchyards, under eaves like wooden eyebrows'.

FIVE

The Later Churches – Eighteenth and Nineteenth Centuries

For 80 years after Wren's death, churches in the Classical tradition were produced in London and up and down the country by Hawksmoor, Archer, Flitcroft, Gibbs, the Dances, etc. But soon after 1800 the Greek and Gothic revival fashions overtook that tradition, which however died reluctantly, especially in the many and varied non-Gothic steeples that arose on every hand until the 1830s.

But in the City there were but few examples of these later churches, as the following exhaustive list (including two of Wren's lifetime but not by him) will testify:

1. *Various Classical*

Holy Trinity Minories (a City parish although the church was just outside). 1706, but the north wall was mediaeval. Destroyed in Second World War

St Mary Woolnoth, 1717–27, Hawksmoor, outstanding

St James, Duke's Place, 1727, demolished 1874

St Botolph, Bishopsgate, 1725–28, said to be by James Gold

St Katherine Coleman, 1734, by one Horne, who later rebuilt Holy Trinity, Guildford. Demolished 1927.

St Botolph, Aldgate, 1744, the elder Dance [136]

All Hallows-on-the-Wall, 1765–67, the younger Dance, outstanding

St Botolph, Aldersgate, c.1754 and 1790, charming interior [121]

St Alphege, 1777, Sir Wm Staines. Demolished 1924 but base of mediaeval tower remains as ruin

St Peter-le-Poer, 1788–92, Jesse Gibson, circular with beautiful domed steeple. Demolished 1908, a great loss

St Martin Outwich, 1796, S.P. Cockerell, oval, demolished 1874

2. *Gothic Revival*

St Dunstan-in-the-East, tower Wren, body of church 1817–21, David Laing. Ruined Second World War. It had a charming interior with all its contemporary fittings including a wondrous pulpit vaulted beneath, and reading desk. Also a painted east window reminiscent of Britton's illustrations of Fonthill Abbey. Another great loss [131].

St Bartholomew-the-Less, octagonal in wood by younger Dance, 1789; rebuilt in stone and iron, 1823, by Hardwick. West end mediaeval, apse much altered. See Godwin & Britton.

St Dunstan-in-the-West, 1831–33, John Shaw. It has a fine steeple, the lantern of which is an almost exact copy of that at All Saints' Pavement, York; and in the way it is united with the tower Shaw has improved on his original. It certainly is an ornament to Fleet Street.

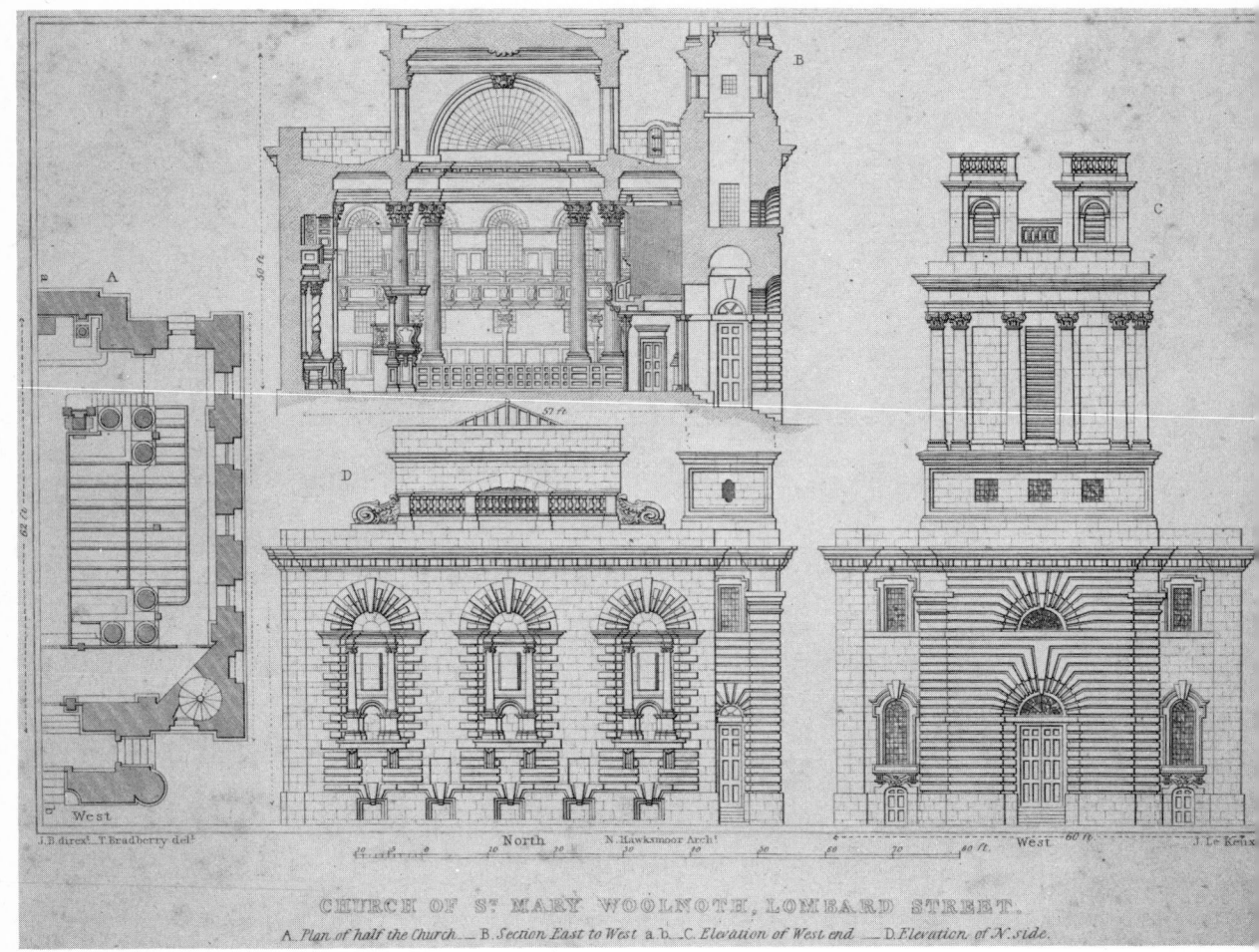

CHURCH OF S.T. MARY WOOLNOTH, LOMBARD STREET.
A. *Plan of half the Church.* — B. *Section East to West* a.b. — C. *Elevation of West end.* — D. *Elevation of N. side.*

115   St Mary Woolnoth: an engraving from *The Public Buildings of London* by Britton and Pugin, Vol 1, 1825

All three churches in this section were covered by plaster groined vaults.

3. 'Norman'

Holy Trinity, Gough Square, 1837–38, John Shaw, junior, architect. In the parish of St Bride. Demolished 1913 [126].

The neglect into which the churches and churchyards fell in the nineteenth century is, allowing for exaggeration, well illustrated by two articles by Charles Dickens in *The Uncommercial Traveller*, published in 1859. In the first he says:

It came into my head one day, here had I been cultivating a familiarity with all the churches of Rome, and I knew nothing of the insides of the old churches of London! This befell on a Sunday morning and I began my expeditions that very same day and they lasted me a year ... I have come to the region of Whittington in an omnibus ... It is twenty minutes short of eleven ... when I stroll down one of the many narrow hilly streets in the City that lead due south to the Thames ... So many bells are ringing ... the discordance is fearful ... As I stand at the street corner, I don't see as many as four people at once going to

116   St Mary Woolnoth, 1716–27

117   St Katherine Coleman, 1739–42

118   St Botolph, Bishopsgate, 1725–29

119   All Hallows-on-the-Wall, built 1765

120   All Hallows-on-the-Wall

121   St Botolph, Aldersgate, built *c*.1790

122   St Peter-le-Poer, Old Broad Street, rebuilt 1792, dem. 1908

123   St Peter-le-Poer, an engraving from *The Public Buildings of London* by Britton and Pugin, Vol II, 1828

124 St Dunstan-in-the-West (re-built 1831): south doorway

125 St Michael Cornhill: Scott's north doorway of 1858

126   Holy Trinity, Gough Square, built 1838, demolished 1913

church, though I see as many as four churches with their steeples clamouring for people. I choose my church and go up a flight of steps to the great entrance in the tower' [St James Garlickhithe?] . . . 'Through a screen of wood and glass I peep into the dim church. About twenty people are discernible, waiting to begin. Christening would seem to have faded out of this church long ago, for the font has the dust of desuetude thick upon it . . . I perceive the altar to be rickety and the Commandments damp. Entering after this survey, I jostle the clergyman in his canonicals, who is entering too from a dark lane behind a pew of state with curtains where nobody sits. The pew is ornamented with four blue wands once carried by four somebodys, I suppose, before somebody else . . . I open the door of a family pew and shut myself in . . . The opening of the service recalls my wandering thoughts. I then find, to my astonishment, that I have been . . . taking a strong kind of invisible snuff, up my nose, into my eyes and down my throat . . . all our little party wink, sneeze and cough. The snuff seems to be made of the decay of matting, wood, cloth, stone, iron, earth and something else. Is the something else, the decay of dead citizens in the vaults below? As sure as Death it is! . . . We stamp our feet to warm them, and dead citizens arise in heavy clouds. . . . Another Sunday . . . I make selection of a church oddly put away in a corner among a number of lanes – a smaller church than the last and an ugly; . . . as a congregation we are fourteen strong; not counting an exhausted charity school in a gallery which has dwindled away to four boys and two girls. In the porch is a benefaction of loaves of bread which there would seem to be nobody left . . . to claim. . . . There is . . . an exhausted clerk in a brown wig and two or three exhausted doors and windows have been bricked up, and the service books are musty, and the pulpit cushions are threadbare, and the whole church furniture is in a very advanced stage of exhaustion. We are three old women (habitual), two young lovers (accidental), two tradesmen, one with a wife and one alone, an aunt and nephew, two girls . . . and three sniggering boys. The clergyman . . . has the moist and vinous

look . . . of one acquainted with 'Twenty port. . . . He does all he has to do in a steady jog-trot, like a farmer's wife going to market . . . and gives us a concise sermon (whose) drowsy cadence soon lulls the three old women to sleep. . . . There are few more striking indications of the changes of manners and customs than these deserted churches. . . . They remain like the tombs of the old citizens who lie beneath them and around them, Monuments of Another Age.

In Pugin and Britton's *Public Buildings of London*, 1825–8, only three of Wren's churches, besides St Paul's are dealt with, and in 1838 Godwin and Britton (*Churches of London*) showed little appreciation of these masterpieces. Of the now demolished St Benet Fink, they say: 'The tower is dwarfish and devoid of beauty; it is surmounted by a dome of indescribable form' (quite untrue, as it was simply square on plan); and of the oval interior: 'It has been pointed out as a fine specimen of its author's genius, but, excepting so far as regards the adaptation of means to circumstances, we can discover little of genius in it. As a whole the composition is crowded and confused, and in the details there is nothing to admire'. And of the charming St Benet, Paul's Wharf: 'The present church was built in the year 1683 from the designs of Sir Christopher Wren, but does not offer any distinguishing features of excellence. Of the interior . . . we are unable to speak more favourably than of the exterior'. And, of the very attractive All Hallows-on-the-Wall the authors say, 'The interior is a monument of bad taste, being not merely inappropriate, but . . . ill designed and very ugly'.

Also, most unfortunately for the churches, at this period the City began to be deserted by its resident inhabitants to become what it is at present – a City of workers who live elsewhere, as Dickens has just shown us. The result was that in 1834 an attempt was made, emanating from the Corporation, to reduce the number of churches – the first of a long series of such attempts. The City Fathers had just demolished St Michael, Crooked Lane, to make way for the new London Bridge; and upon the burning of the Royal Exchange four years later, they appear to have thought that a general tidying up of the City at the expense of 13 of the rapidly-becoming-'superfluous' churches would be a good thing. But on hearing from the bishop that they would be expected to provide for 13 new churches in the suburbs, they dropped the matter, after destroying St Bartholomew-by-the-Exchange and St Benet Fink.

But the evil seed, withering at its first sowing,

127   Pulpit, St Mary Woolnoth

soon found more congenial soil, this time in the Church itself.

Henceforth, it was the bishops themselves who laboured to decimate these beautiful buildings. In 1860 was passed the Union of Benefices Act, the object of which was to facilitate the removal of churches deemed to be superfluous, but requiring the consent, not only of the patron of the Living, but also of the Vestry of any church before it could be demolished. Under it some 22 old churches, 16 of which were Wren's,[1] have been disposed of, 14 in the first 28 years. As if that were not fast enough, Bishop Jackson in 1883, following an earlier attempt of 1876, tried to get passed an Act for speeding up the process of disposal by abolishing the necessity for the Vestry's consent. This happily did not succeed. Further attempts at mass destruction were made, apparently in 1894 and 1899, and after the 1914–18 War Bishop Winnington-Ingram appointed a Commission which in 1919 reported in favour of demolishing 19 churches at once. This aroused a storm of protest and did not get as far as Parliament, but a modified version of it passed the Church Assembly in 1924, and coming before the House of Commons two years later, was signally defeated, the Corporation itself presenting a petition against it at the Bar of the House.

From time to time protests were raised, but seemingly without much effect. One of the earliest is a contribution by Ed. John Carlos to the *Gentleman's Magazine* for May, 1840, protesting against the proposed demolition of St Bartholomew and St Benet Fink. The opening sentence might, with the alteration of a date and a name, almost have been written between the Wars. He says: 'The sweeping design of destroying a number of the City churches which was mediated in . . . 1834, and for the time arrested by the resolute opposition to the measure in the instance of the first church marked out for sacrifice, St Clement Eastcheap, it may be feared is at length coming into full operation, not, indeed in the open

---

[1] These, with the three mentioned above and St Christopher-le-Stocks – crowded out by the Bank of England in 1781 – made a total of 19 of Wren's churches deliberately destroyed and one made over to the Welsh community, St Benet, Paul's Wharf.

manner in which it was displayed at that period, but in an insidious and therefore more secure mode of procedure'. The article ends thus: 'The apathy with which the removal of St Bartholomew's church has been regarded will be remembered and felt when perhaps the loss of this church will be found a trifle in comparison with the wholesale destruction to which, ere long, the churches of the

128 Altarpiece, St Mary Woolnoth

129 Late 18th-century reredos, St Michael Bassishaw

130   St Giles Cripplegate – east window, 1792

131 St Dunstan-in-the-East as rebuilt 1821, with contemporary glass and furniture

132 St Mary Aldermary in 1866, showing organ of 1781

metropolis may chance to be destined.' Alas! how true this has proved to be.

Thomas Carlyle wrote (to the City Churches and Churchyard Protection Society, not founded until 1879, after so many churches had been destroyed): 'my clear feeling is that it would be a sordid, nay, sinful piece of barbarism to do other than religiously preserve these churches as precious heirlooms. Many of them are specimens of noble architecture, the like of which we have no prospect of ever being able to produce again'. Among others who protested were Sir Gilbert Scott (Gothicist though he was), G.E. Street, Holman Hunt, and William Morris.[1]

Of course the view of the Ecclesiastical Commissioners is understandable. Here were nearly 50 parish churches, mostly rich benefices, in the midst of a strictly business community which left them practically deserted on Sundays while the new and ever increasing suburbs were almost without places of worship. What more obvious solution than to pull down the majority of these 'redundant' buildings, sell the immensely valuable sites and with the proceeds build new churches where most needed in outer London? Apart from the artistic and historical sides of the question, the argument had all the backing of logic, common sense and sound business instinct. But is there nothing higher than these? The Commissioners did not sufficiently remember that Sunday is not the only day when a church may be useful, and with 500,000 people seething round their doors, 48 churches were not too many – it worked out at over 10,000 persons per church! And surely the financial centre of the world needed some reminders that successful business is not the Chief End of man. And where there was a live incumbent he found his work in the City a full-time job.

But then in 1939 the Second World War descended on us, at which time the City churches numbered 47, All Hallows, Lombard Street having meanwhile been closed and later demolished. Of these 47, 18 were badly damaged, including 15 of Wren's. Seven of these 47 have now been removed and the rest have been restored, while one has been

taken to the United States. Thus the number of City churches now remaining and in use is 39. But the importance of the City churches on architectural and historical grounds was at last becoming appreciated. After the war, an effort was made by the Church to save and use as many as possible of the City churches by promoting the City of London (Guild Churches) Act, which became law in 1952 and operative in 1954. This Act provided for freeing certain churches from parochial responsibilities and constituting them 'Guild' churches with concern only for weekday congregations and for special forms of religious work. It would, in the words of Dr Wand, then bishop of London, turn the City into 'a great laboratory in which new methods of ministry, new spiritual expedients and new pastoral techniques may be tried out for the benefit of the Church as a whole ... such as religious drama, Christian films, visual aids in religious education, apologetics, religious art and literature'.

Under the Act, provision was made for 15 Guild churches and 24 parish churches but one of the former, St Michael Royal, has since been deprived of its Guild status (see Guide). But in spite of this Act, some churches not badly damaged were allowed to deteriorate, as St Anne and St Agnes, Gresham Street, or even to become derelict as All Hallows, London Wall and St Katherine Cree. But happily, after urgent representation to the bishop, these last three churches have been restored.

Christians should pray for the outpouring of the Holy Spirit in the City so that these historic churches may continue through midday services and study groups etc, to bring the Divine influence to bear upon the problems of the office and the warehouse and so set forward the coming of the Kingdom of God.

Since about 1960 redevelopment of the City has caused the disappearance of many small streets and exposed views of some churches hitherto unobtainable – as for instance the ground between St Helen, Bishopsgate and St Andrew Undershaft, Leadenhall Street which can be seen from the same spot, and even from each other.

---

[1] See letter to *Times* 17.4.1878, quoted by Pevsner in *The Future of the Past* (Thames & Hudson, 1976) p. 52, in which Morris shows amazing appreciation of Wren's churches.

SIX

City Churchyards

Besides the churches, about half of which still retained their yards or portions of them, there were before the last war very many delightful little oases dotted over the City, showing by a few mouldering tombstones that they also were once attached to a church now long since vanished. There were, it is believed, upwards of 70 of these and other green spots amid the wilderness of brick and concrete that made up the City. Churchyards were exempted from the working of the Union of Benefices Act and it required an Act of Parliament to do away with any of them.

But with the drastic redevelopment of the City since the war, a dozen or more have disappeared and it seems likely that more will follow them. Of those that remain several have been transformed into ornamental gardens, especially:

St John Zachary, Gresham Street (greatly enlarged)

St Mary Staining near Wood Street

St Dunstan-in-the-East (old churchyard developed, and enclosed garden in church ruins)

St Mary Aldermanbury (old churchyard and new garden round church foundations)

Of these burial grounds in former times interesting particulars may be gleaned from the parish books etc, which show that they were often used for secular purposes and must have been pleasant spots – except indeed for a year or two after the epidemics of plague which periodically swept over London, culminating in the terrible visitation of 1665, of which the present high levels of some of the churchyards are a mute reminder.

From Stow we learn that in 1370, in consequence of disputes among weavers, it was ordered that the Flemish weavers should meet in St Lawrence Pountney churchyard and the weavers of Brabant in that of St Mary Somerset, for hiring of serving men.

As mentioned before, several of the mediaeval churches had cloisters attached, but it would appear that the term 'cloister' was often applied to a mere covered way in the burial ground, but in three cases it appears to have stood for a regular four-square enclosure, as at St Michael, Cornhill where it surrounded a preaching Cross 'not much unlike Paul's Cross', and at All Hallows-the-Great of which Stow says, 'This is a fair church with a large cloister on the south side thereof, about their churchyard, but foully defaced and ruinated'. Other churches said to have had cloisters were St Katherine Cree, St Martin Outwich, St Mary Aldermanbury, St Mildred, Poultry, St Peter, Cornhill, St Swithun and St Mary Bothaw. At St Magnus in 1663, it is recorded that there was a large cloister passing under the chancel from Thames Street to another cloister on the south side of the church. Over both cloisters are 'ffayre howses and Tenements erected'. One of the few post-Fire cloisters was at St Benet Fink of which the following description from the Gentleman's Magazine for May 1840 is interesting:

> The backs of the houses in Sweetings Rents, taken down for the improvements, abutted on the burying ground attached to this church. These houses were partly built over the church-yard, being sustained on pillars, forming a kind of walk or cloister on one side . . . This mode of building will explain the meaning of cloisters which are so often mentioned by Stow as apper-taining to the parish churches of London as well as the term 'jetty' so often met with in . . . docu-ments relating to the City in its former state. The present colonnade has superseded the ancient cloisters with their superincumbent apartments; and the jetties though in modern times laid into and forming part of the adjacent houses, are, in fact, held under distinct tenures'.

There is a mention of 'cleaning the cloysters' at St Swithun in 1692[1]; at St Mildred, Poultry, the parsonage was built on pillars, forming a cloister beneath; while at St Vedast a pillared passage or cloister still survives (largely renewed) on the north side of the church.

During the Great Plague the yards were soon filled with bodies and orders were given to cover them with 12 inches of unslaked lime and a like quantity of gravel or earth, thus raising the levels as before noted. But overcrowding of the church-yards was not confined to the plague years. At Holy Trinity Minories the smallness of their burial-ground was a constant trouble to the Vestry, and in 1689 and again in 1763 they resorted to the extraordinary expedient of emptying it, but what became of the corpses does not appear! After the Great Fire, the cemeteries and sites of the churches were at night the resort of thieves and footpads, and by day the housewives used them for hanging out their washing!

To remind people of their Latter End, gates to the churchyards were frequently ornamented with gruesome devices. At St Olave, Hart Street skulls were carved impaled on spikes; at St Katherine Cree a recumbent skeleton (now behind the church) filled the pediment, while All Hallows, Lombard Street, was approached through the remarkable doorway shown opposite. But in some parishes a

better outlook prevailed, and a carved Resurrection scene was placed over the entrance, as at St Stephen, Coleman Street,[2] [134] St Mary-at-Hill and St Andrew, Holborn – at the latter church now built into its north wall.

The pleasanter side of these grounds is shown in the following extracts from Churchwardens Ac-counts:

St Mary Woolchurch Haw

1560 Item paid the xxix daye of March for making the Arber in the Churchyard   xvi[d]

1586 Paid to Thomas Addames dwellynge in the Duches place for cutinge and bindinge upe of all the trees in the churchyard   viii[s]

St Stephen Walbrook

1577–8 Item for cutting the hedges in the Church-yard   xii[d]

1604–5 Paid for Cutting the Grasse plot and weed-ing the Allies in ye Churchyard   ii[s]

St Mary Somerset

In 1680 six Elm trees were planted in the burial ground.

St Mildred, Poultry

9th November 1753. Paid for Pruneing the Trees in the Ch. Yd   2s. 6d.

13th February 1754 Paid for Digging and Sowing the Churchyard   5s. 0d.

St Michael, Cornhill

1679 Ap 24 Resolved 'That leave be given to the Parson of St Peters to walk in the Churchyard'

St Michael, Crooked Lane

15 Aug 1773 It was Ordered that an 'umbarello' be provided for use at burials in wet weather. (Hist. of the Church, p. 212)

All Hallows, Barking

J.P. Malcolm (in his *Londinium Redivivum* Vol II, 1803) says that the churchyard, 'within a yard (3 feet) much higher than the pavement' had 'several trees judiciously disposed around it'; and in his description of the interior as 'vener-able, beautiful' and 'solemn' he says 'the win-dows are enlivened by the vivid beams of the sun glancing on the ivy leaf, the lime tree and the

---

[1] White, *Hist. of Walbrook Ward*, 1904, p. 479.

[2] Unfortunately the original carving was taken down and placed in the vestry and a careful copy substituted over the gate. The original perished with the church.

133   Former carved entrance from the street, All Hallows, Lombard Street

134　St Stephen, Coleman Street: original carving (from the street entrance), des. 1940

lilac. Those wave in the wind and transport the spectator to the wild beauties of nature'.
And of St Ethelburga he says 'The Church has a small yard eastwards with poplars surrounding it. It is entirely enclosed by houses'.

In *The Uncommercial Traveller*, Dickens writes:

'Such strange churchyards hide in the City of London; churchyards sometimes so entirely detached from churches, always so pressed upon by houses; so small, so rank, so silent, so forgotten except by the few people who ever look down into them from their smoky windows. As I stand peeping in through the iron gates and rails, I can peel the rusty metal off, like bark from an old tree. The illegible tombstones are all lopsided, the grave-mounds lost their shape in the rains of a hundred years ago . . . One of my best loved churchyards, I call the churchyard of St

Ghastly Grim; . . . It is a small, small churchyard with a ferocious strong spiked iron gate like a jail. This gate is ornamented with skulls and cross-bones, larger than the life, wrought in stone; (and) thrust through and through with iron spears'.

(This is evidently the gate at St Olave, Hart Street.)

After describing how some yards were over-looked by Companies' Halls or surrounded by warehouses, with windows full of bales, he writes:

'Such was the surrounding of one City church-yard that I saw last summer on a Volunteering Saturday evening towards eight of the clock, when with astonishment I beheld an old old man and an old old woman in it making hay . . .! Gravely among the graves, they made hay all alone by themselves. There was but one rake between them, and they both had hold of it in a pastoral-loving manner, and there was hay on the old woman's black bonnet, as if the old man had recently been playful. They looked like Time and his wife . . . The old woman was much too bright for a pew-opener, the old man much too meek for a beadle . . . In another churchyard of similar cramped dimensions, I saw, that self same summer, two comfortable charity children. They were making love – tremendous proof of the vigour of that immortal article, for they were in the graceful uniform under which English Charity delights to hide herself. . . . But such instances, or any tokens of vitality, are rare indeed in my City churchyards. A few sparrows occasionally try to raise a lively chirrup in their solitary tree – perhaps, as taking a different view of worms from that entertained by humanity – but they are flat and hoarse of voice, like the clerk, the organ, the bell, the clergyman and all the rest of the Church-works when they are wound up for Sunday . . . So little light lives inside the churches of my churchyards, when the two are co-existent, that it is often only by accident . . . that I discover their having stained glass in some odd window. The westering sun slants into the churchyard by some unwonted entry, a few prismatic tears drop on an old tombstone, and a window that I thought was only dirty is for the moment all bejewelled. Then the light passes and the colours die.

Though even then, gazing up at the tower, I see the rusty vane new burnished, and seeming to look out with a joyous flash over the sea of smoke at the distant shore of country'.

Some few examples such as these remained up to the last war but most of those now surviving are better cared for, and many are open to the public.

Along Cheapside the cemetery of St Peter Cheap at the corner of Wood Street is famous for its plane tree, which in 1850 contained four rooks' nests.

It is hidden by three tiny houses originally erected by the parish in 1687, which 'were the only surviving examples of the first and least sort of building of two storeys, for by-streets and lanes, authorized by the Rebuilding Act of 1667. Each consists of 2 rooms only'. Fronting Wood Street is a fine iron railing with crossed keys and bust in relief of St Peter, set up in 1712 at a cost of £107. 11. 0d.

Many of the churchyards were provided with an inscribed stone recording the destruction of the church in 'the dreadful Fire of 1666' and examples survived at St John Zachary, St Mary Staining and St Olave, Silver Street – all close together. Sometimes watch-houses were erected to guard the graves from the body-snatchers, as at St Sepulchre (dated 1791), blitzed and now rebuilt, and All Hallows-the-Great and Less. At Holy Trinity Minories there was formerly an attractive churchyard with trees and seats for the parishioners, but it gradually lost its beauty and was paved over in 1771. At St Mary Abchurch the yard is paved with a variety of coloured flagstones and setts which form a pleasant geometric pattern. The three St Botolphs have large burial-grounds, that at Aldersgate being extended to form the 'Postmen's Park', and contains the G.F. Watts Cloister commemorating otherwise unremembered heroes of civil life. At St Botolph Bishopsgate, there is a tennis court. A bisected cemetery marks the site of St Lawrence Pountney. The yards at St Edmund and St Ethelburga have been turned into prim little gardens. The churchyard of St Christopher formed the delightful Garden Court at the Bank of England, now built over.

It was curious how the churchyard trees fared in the great fire 'blitz' of Christmas 1940. They seemed to have miraculously escaped, as every twig was perfect; but the spring showed how delusive this was – they were mostly dead, with the bark shelling right off the trunk, or perhaps only on one side of it, with a line of bright green foliage up the other – in any case a melancholy enough sight.

PART TWO

London City Churches – A Brief Guide

In writing this little Guide, the author has tried to notice in the fewest words the chief items about each church that might be of interest to visitors. Space has precluded reference to the fine Communion plate and Beadles' staves etc. with which the City churches abound – moreover, they are not usually on show.

Also there is nothing said about the Parish Books – Churchwardens Accounts and Vestry Minutes and the Registers, which are full of human interest to the patient enquirer. Many of these are on permanent loan to the Guildhall Library, where they may be inspected.

The times during which the churches are open, vary, but most can be visited around midday (except weekends).

Lists of the Churches

1. *Destroyed before the Great Fire of 1666*

St Mary Magdalen ⎤
St Michael ⎥
St Katherine[1] ⎬
Blessed Trinity ⎦
  Demolished when Holy Trinity Priory, Aldgate
  was built on site of four parishes (Stow), 1108

St Olave, Bread Street
  United to St Nicholas Olave (Kingsford's *Stow*),
  1250

St Faith
  Demolished *c*.1255 for extension of east end of
  St Paul's (but continued using St Paul's crypt
  as 'St Faith under St Paul's')

St Augustine Papey
  Ceased to be parochial 1442, was taken over by
  an almshouse (then founded or refounded) and
  demolished under Edward VI, 1547–1553

St Audoen or Ewin ⎤ remains recently
St Nicholas-in-the-Shambles ⎦ uncovered
  Absorbed by new parish of Christ Church,
  Newgate Street, 1547, and thereafter demolished

St Mary Axe
  United to St Andrew Undershaft in 1565, and
  thereafter demolished

2. *Destroyed 1666 and not rebuilt*

Holy Trinity the Less
All Hallows, Honey Lane
All Hallows-the-Less
St Andrew Hubbard
St Anne Blackfriars
St Benet Sherehog
St Botolph, Billingsgate
St Faith under St Paul's
St Gabriel Fenchurch
St Gregory by St Paul's
St John the Baptist on Walbrook
St John the Evangelist
St John Zachary
St Lawrence Pountney
St Leonard Eastcheap (remains recently uncovered)
St Leonard Foster
St Margaret Moses

---

[1] Stow says that the four parishes became one parish of the
Blessed Trinity – but it seems St Katherine parish continued
to exist, the parishioners apparently using part of Holy Trinity
Priory until the thirteenth century when the predecessor of the
present St Katherine Cree was built for them. (See Kingsford's
Stow, Vol 1, pp. 140 and 291 – supplement, 7 – also London
Topographical Record, Vol V, p. 55.)

St Margaret, New Fish Street
St Martin Orgar
   (Although united to St Clement Eastcheap, it
   was repaired and used by French Protestants
   until 1820)
St Martin Pomary
St Martin Vintry
St Mary Bothaw
   (Part of east wall remained until Cannon Street
   Station was built)
St Mary Colechurch
St Mary Mounthaw
St Mary Staining
St Mary Woolchurch Haw
St Mary Magdalen, Milk Street
St Michael-le-Querne
St Nicholas Acons
St Nicholas Olave
St Olave, Silver Street
St Pancras, Soper Lane
St Peter, Paul's Wharf
St Peter Westcheap
St Thomas Apostle

3.   *Churches demolished from 1781–1939*
St Christopher-le-Stocks   1781
St Michael, Crooked Lane   1831
St Bartholomew-by-the-Exchange   1841
St Benet Fink   1846
St Benet Gracechurch   1867
All Hallows Staining   1870 (tower remains)
St Mary Somerset   1871 (tower remains)
St Mildred, Poultry   1872
St James, Duke's Place   1874
St Martin Outwich   1874
St Michael Queenhithe   1876
St Antholin   1875 (Tower 1876)
All Hallows, Bread Street   1877
St Dionis Backchurch   1878
St Matthew, Friday Street   1885
St Olave Jewry   1887 (tower remains)
St Mary Magdalen, Old Fish Street   Burnt, 1886,
   Dem, 1890
All Hallows-the-Great   Tower and N. aisle, 1876,
   church, 1894
St Michael, Wood Street   1897
St Michael Bassishaw   1900
St George, Botolph Lane   1904

St Peter-le-Poer   1908
Holy Trinity, Gough Square   (Built 1831) 1913
St Alphege   1924 (mediaeval tower remains as
   ruin)
St Katherine Coleman   1926
All Hallows, Lombard Street   1939 (tower rebuilt
   at Twickenham, 1940)

4.   *Churches wrecked in 1939–45 war and since
demolished or not to be rebuilt*
Christ Church, Newgate Street
   Tower, west end, and north wall remain,
   enclosing garden
St Alban, Wood Street
   Ruins demolished – tower remains
St Augustine, Watling Street
   Ruins demolished – tower remains incorporated
   in St Paul's Choir School, 1967
St Dunstan-in-the-East
   Tower and ruins remain, latter incorporated in
   public garden
St Mildred, Bread Street
   Ruins and part of tower remained until 1972
St Stephen, Coleman Street
   Ruins demolished
St Swithun, Cannon Street
   Ruins demolished

5.   *Church remaining but not in London*
St Mary Aldermanbury
   Now at Fulton, Missouri, U.S.A.

6.   *Churches remaining and in use in City*
All Hallows, Barking
All Hallows, London Wall
St Andrew, Holborn
St Andrew Undershaft
St Andrew-by-the-Wardrobe
St Anne & St Agnes
St Bartholomew-the-Great
St Bartholomew-the-Less
St Benet's Welsh Church
St Botolph Aldersgate
St Botolph, Aldgate
St Botolph, Bishopsgate
St Bride, Fleet Street
St Clement Eastcheap
St Dunstan-in-the-West

St Edmund, Lombard Street
St Ethelburga
St Giles Cripplegate
St Helen, Bishopsgate
St James Garlickhithe
St Katherine Creechurch
St Lawrence Jewry
St Magnus London Bridge
St Margaret, Lothbury
St Margaret Pattens
St Martin, Ludgate
St Mary Abchurch
St Mary Aldermary
St Mary-at-Hill
St Mary-le-Bow
St Mary Woolnoth
St Michael, Cornhill
St Michael Royal
St Nicholas Cole Abbey
St Olave, Hart Street
St Peter, Cornhill
St Sepulchre
St Stephen Walbrook
St Vedast
Austin Friars
Temple Church

7. *Wren Churches*
Christ Church, Newgate Street
  B 1940, T to stay,[1] R remain
All Hallows, Bread Street
  Dem 1877
All Hallows, Lombard Street
  Dem 1939 – T rebuilt Twickenham
All Hallows-the-Great
  T dem 1876 – church 1894
St Alban, Wood Street
  B 1940, R dem, T remains
St Andrew, Holborn
  B 1941, Res 1961
St Andrew-by-the-Wardrobe
  B 1940, Res 1961
St Anne & St Agnes
  B 1940, Res 1966
St Antholin, Watling Street
  Body dem 1875, T 1876
St Augustine Old Change
  B 1941, R dem, T remains

St Bartholomew-by-the-Exchange
  Dem 1841
St Benet Fink
  Dem 1846
St Benet Gracechurch
  Dem 1876
St Benet, Paul's Wharf
  since 1879, Welsh Church
St Bride, Fleet Street
  B 1940, Res 1957
St Christopher-le-Stocks
  Dem 1781
St Clement Eastcheap
  minor dam
St Dionis Backchurch
  Dem 1878
St Dunstan-in-the-East[2]
  B 1941, T and R to stay
St Edmund King & Martyr
  Dam 1917 and 1941
St George, Botolph Lane
  Dem 1904
St James Garlickhithe
  Dam 1941, Res 1963
St Lawrence Jewry
  B 1940, Res 1957
St Magnus, London Bridge
  minor dam
St Margaret, Lothbury
  Undam
St Margaret Pattens
  Undam
St Martin, Ludgate
  Undam
St Mary Abchurch
  Dam 1940 and later
St Mary Aldermanbury
  Wrecked 1940 – re-erected at Fulton, Missouri
  U.S.A. 1966–69)
St Mary Aldermary
  Minor dam
St Mary-at-Hill
  Undam
St Mary-le-Bow
  B 1941, fully Res 1964

[1] Spire rebuilt, 1958–59.
[2] Rebuilt (except tower) by Laing, 1817–21 – Spire rebuilt, 1953.

St Mary Somerset
  Dem except T 1871
St Mary Magdalen
  B 1886, Dem 1890
St Matthew, Friday Street
  Dem 1885
St Michael Bassishaw
  Dem 1900
St Michael, Cornhill
  Undam
St Michael, Crooked Lane
  Dem 1831
St Michael Queenhithe
  Dem 1876
St Michael Royal
  Dam by flying bombs 1944. Res 1968
St Michael, Wood Street
  Dem 1897
St Mildred, Bread Street
  Blasted 1941, now Dem
 St Mildred, Poultry
  Dem 1872
St Nicholas Cole Abbey
  Bombed 1941, Res 1962

St Olave Old Jewry
  Dem except T 1887
St Peter, Cornhill
  Undam
St Sepulchre, Holborn
  Undam
St Stephen, Coleman Street
  B 1940 – R Dem
St Stephen Walbrook
  Badly dam 1941 – Res 1954
St Swithun, Cannon Street
  B 1941 – R Dem
St Vedast, Foster Lane
  B 1940 – Res 1962

Wren also built 3 other London churches
St Anne, Soho
  Destroyed in War, except T
St Clement Danes
  B now Res
St James, Piccadilly
  B now Res

Notes on the Churches

p. indicates a Parish Church
G. indicates a Guild Church
w. indicates a Ward Church

CHRIST CHURCH, NEWGATE STREET Wren 1677–91, steeple 1703/4.

Burnt out December 1940, after which services were for a time at St Botolph, Aldersgate. Founded by Henry VIII in the church of the newly-dissolved Greyfriars monastery in place of two churches, St Ewin and St Nicholas-in-the-Shambles, which were thereafter pulled down and whose parishes were absorbed by the new parish of Christ Church. The old church was 300 ft long, second only in length to old St Paul's. Present church on site of choir only, the nave being represented by church-yard now a garden. Until 1902 Christ's Hospital (Public School now at Horsham, Sussex) stood alongside, the church being used by the 'Bluecoat Boys'. Huge galleries for their use were provided by Wren, which made it an inferno when the church was burnt in the war. The finely carved font cover was saved by a postman who snatched it to safety (now at St Sepulchre's).

Plans to convert into a church institute and later as a Diocesan H.Q. have been abandoned and the church partly demolished except for the fine steeple. The spire was rebuilt in 1958–59 and 12 urns set on the middle storey to replace the original ones removed early last century.

P. ALL HALLOWS BARKING-BY-THE-TOWER Pre-Fire.

Wrecked in 1941, now rebuilt. 'Barking' refers to its possession in early times by the Abbey of Barking, Essex (founded *c*.675). Of pre-Conquest foundation, proved by the discovery, when the church was bombed, of a late 7th-century doorway at base of tower, believed to be, apart from founda-tions found at St Bride's, the only known Saxon work remaining in a City church. Parts of a late Saxon carved churchyard cross were also found, and in 1951, beneath the nave was discovered the top part of a memorial cross of similar date which showed traces of colour. These and many other items of interest, including a Roman tessellated pavement, fine church plate and record books, etc., are displayed in the crypt (constructed 1926), the east end of which is fitted up as a funerary chapel or columbarium, with stone altar stated to have come from Castle Aihlit, Palestine.

West half of church was supported by massive round thirteenth-century(?) pillars, eastern half by lighter fifteenth-century ones. Had fine Jacobean pulpit (compare St Helen's) of which the door survives as litany desk, handsome reredos, plain but elegant font with exquisite cover (cupids stealing grapes), by Grinling Gibbons[1] (removed

---

[1] Churchwardens Accounts, 1682.

to safety and now carefully cleaned and repaired),[1] brass altar rails (now mostly renewed), splendid seventeenth-century altar-table and fine organ by Renatus Harris, both destroyed in the last war and closely copied in present organ case and table. The fine ironwork of the reading desk originally supported the handrail to the Jacobean pulpit. The tower, after a nearby explosion of gunpowder, was rebuilt in 1659 and up this went Samuel Pepys to view devastation after the Great Fire of 1666.

The headless body of Archbishop Laud was buried here 1645. In 1663 it was removed to chapel of his Oxford college, St John's. William Penn, founder of Pennsylvania was here baptised, 1644, and J. Quincy Adams, later President, U.S.A., here married Louisa Catherine Johnson.

Porch rebuilt *c*.1885 and room over it, now a chapel, was used for parish worship from 1941 until N. aisle of church was restored and rehallowed 14 July 1949. The many fine monuments on north and south walls of church survived the blitz, including two canopied Gothic tombs in N.E. and S.E. corners. The former (badly damaged in the war) commemorates Alderman John Croke with two brasses of himself, wife and children, 1477. The E. end of this N. aisle is Chapel of TOC H (founded by former incumbent, Rev. P. B. Clayton ('Tubby' Clayton) during the 1914–18 War) and on Croke tomb is casket containing ever-burning Toc H lamp, given in 1922 by H.R.H. Duke of Windsor when Prince of Wales. Nearby is First World War memorial by Cecil Thomas with effigy of Arthur Henry Forster (died of wounds, 1919). The fine series of 17 brasses (including Croke), dating from 1389–1651, were protected by asphalt in war and are all at E. end of church – rubbing is permitted, but only after written application to the verger and parish clerk.

At E. end of south aisle are two tiny crypts, now St Francis' Chapel and oratory of St Clare, and above them the Mariners' Chapel with new semi-elliptical communion table and altar rails (cf. those at St Stephen Walbrook). At west end of south aisle note group of four charming figures representing Mother Love, designed by John Robinson.

The Church itself was rebuilt in a kind of Gothic with irregularly spaced arcades following old foundations, and opened 23 July 1957. It retains the old side walls and its eastern gable derives from the Great Hall at Hampton Court Palace; beneath this is a carving of Toc H lamp and angels by Cecil Thomas. On the tower was erected in 1958 a slender copper-covered spire, the first shaped spire in the City since Wren's time. These works were designed by the late Lord Mottistone. The Wren pulpit comes from St Swithun London Stone.

The painting of the Last Supper beneath enormous E. window is by Brian Thomas and the wealth of heraldic glass in side windows – royalty, private persons, companies, shipping line badges, etc – is by the late Farrar Bell and his son M. Farrar Bell. Ornament on heating apparatus in main arches copied from door of old pulpit.

G.   ALL HALLOWS, LONDON WALL Early foundation, rebuilt 1765, by the younger Dance.
Damaged in last war. Services then held in parish room nearby. Church restored 1962. In mediaeval times All Hallows was famous for its 'ankers' (anchorites) who dwelt close by. Dance's church has attractive steeple and had a charming interior, now happily reinstated. Pulpit only entered from vestry, which is built on foundations of bastion of City Wall. Bowl of font came from St Mary Magdalen, Old Fish Street. After war damage and long neglect the restoration of All Hallows was undertaken by David Nye. It is now occupied by the Council for Places of Worship and until 1972 it was used for exhibitions of Church Art. The chancel is fitted up as a chapel for occasional services and the nave is a library.

G.   ST ANDREW, HOLBORN Escaped Great Fire, but rebuilt 1684–92 and approved by Wren. Tower, 1704. Burnt out 1941.
Services then held in St Andrew's Court House alongside. Church now restored. Early foundation. West end and lower part of tower pre-Fire (note Gothic arches and window). Tower has most elaborate windows, and turrets like Roman altars. Restored by Lord Mottistone, unfortunately without the vanes to the tower pinnacles, almost certainly an original feature. Re-opened 25 October

---

[1] This and the new font now in charming baptistery at w. end. Window by Keith New.

1961, the interior as before, but without gilding until 1975 when it was redecorated in white, buff, green, and black, with much gold.

The carved organ case in a west gallery, chaste white marble font and wooden pulpit are from the old Foundling Hospital Chapel, while in a recess at the west end is the tomb of Thomas Coram, founder of the Hospital – also from the Chapel. The figure of a weeping boy was formerly, with another, now gone, on monument to Thos Manningham, rector and bishop of Chichester (died 1722). Parts of this and other monuments, long lost sight of, were discovered in the crypt, and are now repaired and replaced in the church.

Two new memorials were erected in 1974 to replace those destroyed in the 1939–45 war. One to Dr Sacheverell, rector, 1713–24, who was buried in the chancel, the other to Wm. Marsden, surgeon, founder of the Royal Free Hospital, 1828 (which was removed to Hampstead in 1974).

Benjamin Disraeli was baptized in St Andrew's in 1817.

The fifteenth-century vestibule beneath the tower is a startling contrast to the restored church – its northern extension is tastefully fitted up as a small chapel with a charming reredos and rails from St Luke, Old Street and a panel of stained glass of the Holy Dove, by Brian Thomas. He also designed the six-light east window of the church, showing the Last Supper and the Ascension, with Arms of Queen Anne and Thavies Inn, reminiscent of the former late seventeenth and early eighteenth-century glass in the three east windows, tragically destroyed in the 1939–45 war.

Note moving example of modern embroidery, a long banner of the Crucifixion by Molly Arnold.

Outside, notice 'Resurrection Stone', built into north wall of church (others at St Mary-at-Hill, St Stephen, Coleman Street[1] and St Giles-in-the-Field) and, each side of the tower door, figures of a boy and girl, from the former parochial school in Hatton Garden (now converted into offices), where is a second pair.

West end of Church exposed, 1968, by demolition of buildings facing Holborn Circus, a garden now occupying the site. Exterior of church cleaned, 1970.

P. ST ANDREW UNDERSHAFT, Leadenhall Street. Pre-Fire.

First mentioned before mid-twelfth-century. Name derived from tall shaft or maypole which until 1517 was set up each Mayday outside the church and overtopped it; it was eventually chopped up and burnt as an object of superstition. Church rebuilt 1520–32 – typical of its period. Tower fifteenth-century below (with fine door and knocker); Victorian at top. The handsome nave ceiling was rebuilt 1950 with the old bosses put back. Aisle roofs original. Font by Nicholas Stone, 1631; very fine Wren-period pulpit and iron altar-rails, and organ by Renatus Harris, with its beautiful case – now unhappily removed to east end of south aisle, where its top is hidden. The fine glass in west window (until 1875, in east window) has figures of Edward VI, Elizabeth I, James I, Charles I,[2] and William III (or originally Charles II?), seventeenth-century with Royal Arms and Badges, etc, below, apparently Victorian, as lithograph of *c*.1840 (in church) shows only patterns (inserted *c*.1830, when a splendid Wren-period reredos was demolished).

Contributors to rebuilding of 1520–32 commemorated by Arms in tracery of aisle windows – removed to safety in last war, only six of them have been put back; the rest, still in crates, await reinstatement.

In 1724–25, church was elaborately decorated with monochrome paintings at expense of a Mr Henry Tombes. The ceiling over altar showed the Heavenly Choir and the sides of chancel were painted with a rustic basement (thereon, reclining figures) supporting a Corinthian building with landscape and architecture beyond. Between the clerestory windows were the twelve apostles, while in the spandrels of the main arcade were depicted scenes of the life of Our Lord. Since 1875, all that remain are the latter. After long neglect ten of these have now been cleaned, six on north side and four on south side – the two eastern ones show St Mary (N) and St Luke (S) – no doubt the

[1] See note, p. 130.

[2] These four, given by Sir Christopher Clitheroe, Lord Mayor 1637, at cost of £4. (a mistake for £40?) (*New View of London*, 1708).

spandrels next to the east wall had St Matthew and St John.

Note five semi-Gothic seats in north aisle; three smaller, with paintings of St Andrew, two larger, dated 1841.

There are several brasses and many very fine monuments, including those of several Lord Mayors, three of them also Presidents of Christ's Hospital[1]: Sir Thomas Offley, died 1582, Sir Hugh Hammersley, died 1636 (*c*.10′ high!) and Sir Christopher Clitheroe, died 1642.[2]

Last, but most interesting of all, note monument in north east corner of church, to John Stow, London's first historian (died 1605). Lord Mayor annually renews pen in the effigy's hand at special service. Interior now being repaired after fire in January 1976.

ST ANDREW-BY-THE-WARDROBE, Blackfriars. Wren, 1685–95.
Burnt out December, 1940. Early foundation. Curious name derives from proximity of the King's Great Wardrobe or Storehouse; established in time of Edward III of which Wardrobe Place, Carter Lane, is a reminder. First mentioned *c*.1244. The celebrated preacher, Rev. Wm. Romaine, was rector here 1766–95. In the time of his successor, Rev. Wm. Goode, the newly founded Church Missionary Society held its early meetings in a room of the rectory (still standing) on St Andrew's Hill. After the blitz, services were held in St Anne's Vestry Hall, Church Entry. Church now restored by Marshall Sisson, who greatly improved exterior by removing Victorianisms – vanes, decorations to tower windows and fussy south doorway. Rehallowed 14 July 1961. Interior plain but dignified with piers and ceiling closely copied from the former ones. Galleries open to the church but aisles beneath them enclosed – that on south containing side-chapel and vestries. Note Wren-period pulpit (beautifully cleaned) and font and cover from St Matthew, Friday Street, (dem. 1885) and finely carved Stuart Royal Arms from St Olave Old Jewry[3] (dem. 1888), also fine modern woodwork. In west gallery is an eighteenth-century chamber organ and in west window is a stained glass panel of the conversion of St Paul, also eighteenth-century, while in the chapel and vestries of the south aisle are four

stained glass windows by Carl Edwards. Weather vane, erected 1968, on south-west corner of tower, came from steeple of St Michael Bassishaw (dem. 1900).

ST ANNE AND ST AGNES, Gresham Street. Base of tower fourteenth-century. Wren, 1676–87.
Partly burnt out December, 1940; First mention about 1200 (R.C.H.M., *The City*, 1929). Exterior attractive with symmetrical design on three sides, each with large central window. Note vane on turret topped with large A. Internal cruciform arrangement with four columns – see also St Martin, Ludgate and St Mary-at-Hill. After long neglect the church was offered to a Russian congregation, but refused. It was cleaned and opened for a time and its restoration urged by the Royal Fine Art Commission and the Council for the Care of Churches. It is now restored under Martin Smith for use by Latvian and Lithuanian congregations and was rehallowed 23 April 1966.

The original font and cover, with the sword-rest, plate, etc, are now at St Vedast, but St Anne & St Agnes retains its own west doorcase and fine reredos (unfortunately stained black), besides much good furniture from other churches. The statues of an angel on south doorcase and Father Time on west doorcase, the beautiful and unusual font cover[4] and the Lion and Unicorn come from St Mildred, Bread Street; paintings of Moses and Aaron from St Michael, Wood Street (dem. 1897); and very fine Royal Arms of Charles II from St Mary Whitechapel (destroyed in last war), while the pulpit incorporates three surviving panels from St Augustine, Watling Street pulpit.

P. ST BARTHOLOMEW-THE-GREAT, Smithfield. Pre-Fire.
This grand Norman priory church, now parochial and the oldest in London, was founded for Austin Canons in 1123 by Rahere, a courtier of Henry I, as the outcome of a pilgrimage to Rome. At the same

---

[1] Now at Horsham.
[2] Sir William Craven (Lord Mayor, 1610 and President of Christ's Hospital) was buried here, but without monument.
[3] Gift from rector of St Margaret, Lothbury.
[4] A new font has now been made to fit it – similar to that destroyed with St Mildred, but without ornament.

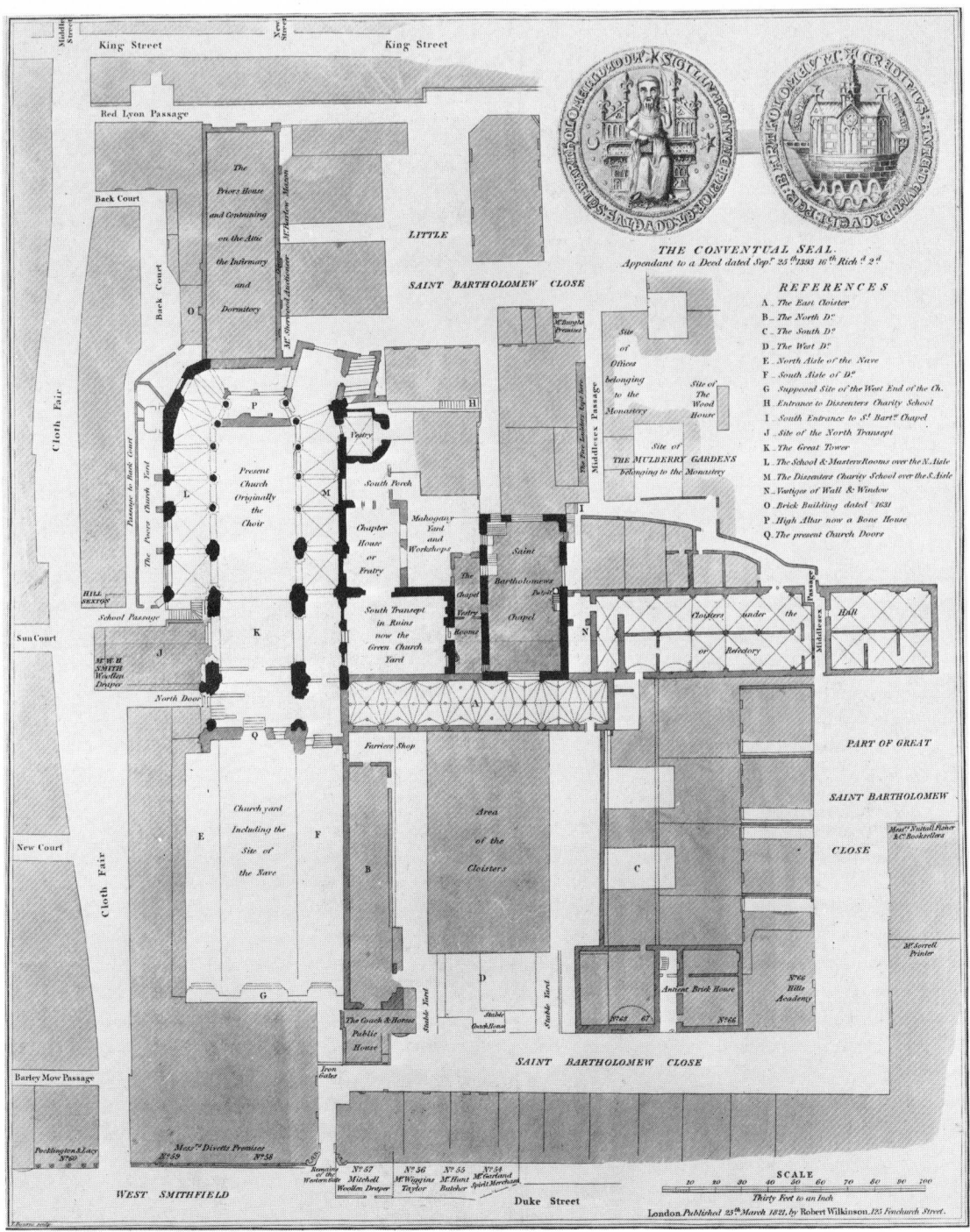

135   St Bartholomew-the-Great in 1821 from an engraving in Wilkinson's *Londina Illustrata*

time he founded the nearby hospital now world-famous as 'Barts'. Formerly buried among secular buildings and, except for west front, almost invisible, St Bartholomew-the-Great consists of the original choir and crossing of the old priory church, with later Lady Chapel at east end over a crypt, and south doorway of original west front (thirteenth-century) remaining as the entrance from Smithfield[1] (over which is an old house formerly the rectory). The Norman work is exceedingly fine, but the apse is a restoration, the transepts are rebuildings and the porches are modern, by Sir Aston Webb, who also arranged his west screen, organ (now with pulpit beneath) and seating as a cathedral choir, restored the Lady Chapel and designed the fine iron screen, made by Starkie Gardner, 1896–97.[2] Note fine crossing piers and arches (semi-circular, east and west; pointed, north and south) with carved decoration of small arches and square flowers high up in the four corners. In the seventeenth-century brick tower are five mediaeval bells. Notice picturesque bay window in south triforium erected by Prior Bolton (1502–32) with his 'rebus', a bolt (or arrow) piercing a tun.

Many fine monuments, especially that of Rahere the founder (north of altar), inscribed in Latin: 'Here lies Rahere, first canon and first prior of this church'. Note little kneeling monks on each side holding books inscribed with verses from Isaiah, also angel holding priory arms. In south aisle is tomb of Sir Walter Mildmay (1589), founder of Emmanuel College, Cambridge. Note also charming tablet to Elizabeth Freshwater near font (which is only mediaeval one in the City). The east walk of the cloisters has been rebuilt on old foundations (key with verger). East end of south aisle, fitted up as Chapel of Imperial Society of Knights Bachelor, dedicated by bishop of London in presence of Her Majesty the Queen, 11 July 1968. Benjamin Franklin worked as a printer's assistant in the Lady Chapel, then in secular occupation – there was a fringe factory in the west part, projecting into the church over the altar until 1885 and, until 1892 a forge on site of north transept (see calcined state of the arches between it and choir).

P. ST BARTHOLOMEW-THE-LESS. Partly pre-Fire, partly rebuilt.

In 'Barts' hospital to which it serves as chapel, although (since Henry VIII's time) parochial in status. Tower and west end fifteenth-century, rest rebuilt 1823 by Hardwick, who preserved unusual octagonal form first given in 1789 by Dance within the old walls. Interior of tower unusual, with its steps, recesses and its banded columns. In vestry, note small brass to William Markeby and his wife, 1439, and on west wall a sixteenth-century canopied altar-tomb, with inscribed slab to John Freke, surgeon, and his wife, mid-eighteenth-century with their impaled arms clumsily fixed to the canopy. On the north wall, two heraldic carvings, with angels (the upper crowned), holding shields of, above, an unidentified arms, and below, a Royal Arms – Edward Confessor impaled with France and England, quarterly – probably for King Henry VI. These, and two others, were on exterior south wall of church until the rebuilding of 1823. On north wall of church note monument to wife of Sir Thomas Bodley, founder of the famous library at Oxford. Inigo Jones, the celebrated architect, was baptized here, 1573. Church opened after restoration and new stained glass by Hugh Easton, unveiled January 1951.[3] At south end of east wall new doorway opened for accommodation of wheeled chairs, 1969.

G. ST BENET'S WELSH CHURCH, Upper Thames Street. Wren, 1677–85, formerly St Benet, Paul's Wharf.

First mention 1111. Very attractive exterior: fine brickwork, carved festoons over windows, hipped roofs over north aisle, and charming steeple. Note sounding-board of pulpit on ceiling of porch. Inside church, the handsome galleries form a rare feature in the City since the raids. On N wall, notice curious substitutes, consisting of palm-branches, shells and cherub-heads, for the Corinthian capitals of pillars and pilasters round rest of the walls. Also

---

[1] Decayed mouldings renewed Nov. 1966.
[2] For similar ironwork, see in depressed arches between north transept and choir 1893, and the much later churchyard gates.
[3] Windows of apse have, centre, Virgin and Child, left, St Luke, and right, St Bartholomew and Rahere.

the fine reredos, elaborate communion table upheld by four angels, with central figure of Charity, inlaid top and carved text along its edge,[1] elegant font and cover and splendid Royal Arms (Charles II) over fine doorway.

In the sixteenth century, Doctors' Commons (dem. 1867 and now defunct, but formerly comprising several Ecclesiastical Courts and the Court of Admiralty) on w. side of Godliman Street and the College of Arms, on E. side of Godliman Street, came to the parish, and the N. gallery was used by them. Its front carries three shields – Royal Arms in the centre (painted with arms of 1816–37), probably for the College of Arms, an office under the Crown[2]: between archbishopric of Canterbury, for the Ecclesiastical Courts, and the Fouled Anchor for the Court of Admiralty. Also, the College of Physicians was founded in the parish in 1518 – at the Great Stone House of Dr Linacre, physician to Henry VII and Henry VIII, and St Benet contains many monuments to officials of the Commons and the two colleges. The earliest memorial in St Benet is on s. wall to Sir Robert Wyseman, dean of the Arches, with bust. Note also the curious monument in S.E. corner of church to Mark and Alice Cottle. On east wall is a tablet to John Charles Brooke, Somerset Herald, who was crushed to death in 1794 at the old Haymarket Theatre on occasion of a Royal visit. Inigo Jones[3] was buried here in 1652 and Henry Fielding, the novelist, here married his second wife, 1747. Since 1879 St Benet has ceased to be parochial and is used by Welsh Episcopalians. The church was restored some years ago by Godfrey Allen, who renewed lead coverings to dome and lantern-roof, etc. Unfortunately the pillars of the interior, which up till then retained their old-time yellow marbling, were painted white.

Following incendiary damage, 1971, St Benet has been finely restored by J.R. Stammers; and was re-dedicated by the bishop of London, 18 May 1973. In that year the church became completely isolated following recent demolitions.

G.W. ST BOTOLPH, ALDERSGATE. Rebuilt, it seems, in two stages, 1754 (N. and E. walls) and 1787–91 (rest of church).
One of four churches formerly by London City gates, dedicated to this Saxon saint. Three of these, still existing, escaped the Great Fire and were rebuilt in the eighteenth century. St Botolph, Aldersgate mentioned time of Henry I (1100–1135). Present church plain to baldness outside (except east end – rebuilt and set back 1831, leaving narrow passage behind altar) but interior dating from *c.*1788, really charming, with its east and west apses, organ in right place in the latter, galleries, fine pulpit and beautiful sanctuary with panels of the four evangelists and painted window of the Agony in the Garden, by J. Pearson, 1788. The present altar-table dated 1639, was displaced *c.*1787 by the Chippendale table now in the west vestibule, only to be reinstated in the restoration of 1872.

A number of fine monuments survive from the old church; note especially Tudor tomb, east end of south aisle, to Dame Ann Packington (d. 1563) with brasses of herself, child and husband. Much late-nineteenth-century glass and, in south aisle, four windows of historical designs (post-war).

Churchyard (formerly divided between three parishes – St Botolph, Christ Church and St Leonard Foster), often known as Postmen's Park, contains G.F. Watts Cloister, with tablets commemorating acts of heroism in humble life. St Botolph's is Centre for After Care of Prisoners.

P. ST BOTOLPH, ALDGATE. Rebuilt 1741–4 by the elder Dance.
Probably of Saxon origin but first mentioned 1115. Church runs north and south with altar at the north. Conspicuous steeple. Interior altered by Bentley, architect of Westminster cathedral, who embellished ceiling with 'art nouveau' plaster angels holding allusive shields of arms. Following a fire in 1965, the church was restored under Rodney Tatchell and the handsome reredos redecorated, the fine font and cover removed from under the south gallery and placed under the tower, where two interesting monuments to Thomas Darcy of

---

[1] ALL THAT LOOK IN LOVE SING PRHISES (sic) TO THE GOD ABOVE THAT CAN INCREASE YOUR LOVE.

[2] There is a shield with supporters of the College of Arms on the E. wall (N. side).

[3] See St Bartholomew-the-Less.

136   St Botolph-without-Aldgate, as restored after fire 1966

the North[1] and Robert Dow (d. 1612), formerly in the galleries, and a new memorial to Sir John Cass (d. 1718) were placed in three niches, with lists of rectors and aldermen on two plaques between them. Also a sacristy was formed at east end of south aisle with screen incorporating balustrades formerly round font. Note handsome metal altar-rails.[2] The otherwise plain pulpit of *c*.1745 is of great interest for its five inlaid panels: (i) chalice receiving three drops of blood from rays, (ii) flaming heart with irradiated triangle, (iii) open Bible beneath dove with outspread wings, (iv) I.H.S. in rayed glory, (v) mitre with coronet. Spire was truncated after the war, but is now made good. The crypt is used as a youth club and centre for rehabilitating 'down and outs'.

P. ST BOTOLPH, BISHOPSGATE. Rebuilt 1725–9 by James Gold.

Earliest mention 1213. Steeple of present church at east end, the chancel being under it. Interior Victorianized. In chancel is a memorial to Sir Paul Pindar (1565–1650), ambassador and financier. Note memorial tablets on jambs of chancel arch, 1700 (N), 1658 (S) and large paintings of the Agony in the Garden and the Walk to Emmaus, each side of the chancel, in memory of a vestry clerk 1892. Edward Alleyn, actor and founder of Dulwich College, baptized in old church, 1566, while John Keats, poet, was baptized in present building, 1795. Fine sword-rest opposite pulpit. Chancel redecorated and re-lit 1968, with fine hanging behind free-standing altar. Large churchyards. Note former church school (remarkable for its date, 1861) to west of church with figures of boy and girl. It was opened in 1952 as Hall of Fan-Makers' Company by its Royal Freeman, H.R.H. The Duchess of Gloucester.

P. ST BRIDE, FLEET STREET. Wren 1670–84, spire 1701–3.

Burnt out December, 1940. Restored 1957. Bride is a corruption of Bridget, a 6th-century Irish saint. First mention time of Henry II (1154–89).[3] The old church was a fine mediaeval building with lofty pinnacled tower on south side. Wren gave the rebuilt church a symmetrical exterior with the highest and one of the most beautiful of his many steeples and a handsome interior, now alas destroyed. The spire, which is a subtle essay in repetitions, was struck by lightning in 1764 and shattered – a lively public controversy on lightning conductors resulting. Wynkin de Worde the early printer and Richard Lovelace were buried in the old church and Samuel Richardson, author of *Pamela*, in the present one (1761), while Samuel Pepys, the world famous diarist, was baptized here, 1633. Latterly St Bride has become 'the Journalists' Church'. After the blitz, services were carried on in the eighteenth-century vestry.

Before rebuilding the church, extensive excavations were conducted by the Roman and Mediaeval London Excavation Council. The foundations were fully explored and now form an extensive crypt, half of which is open to the public. A Roman pavement was discovered at the east end[4] and plans of successive churches back to early Saxon or maybe Roman times were recovered and the development of St Bride from a simple unaisled nave and chancel of 6th-century date, with later apse, to a nave with north aisle and detached south tower and chancel with chapels north and south, of fifteenth century, is clearly marked by actual remains. Aided by exhibits of many kinds dug up in the ruins – carved and moulded stones, coins, tiles, pottery, coffins, gravestones, etc – and prints, drawings, photographs and articles, this slice of London history outside the walls is vividly, perhaps uniquely, brought before us. Two chapels have been fitted up, one under the sanctuary and a tiny vaulted one in the north-east corner. The great newspaper and publishing houses of the district contributed largely to the rebuilding under Godfrey Allen, and the church was rehallowed 19 December 1957, in presence of H.M. The Queen. Seating is collegiate in arrangement, the side aisles being shut out by backs of stalls and furnished only with chairs. Reredos is freely copied from

---

[1] This monument also commemorates Sir Nicholas Carew (who with Darcy was beheaded on Tower Hill, 1538) and others related to them.

[2] Others at St Magnus, St Mary Woolnoth and St Sepulchre.

[3] St Bride was one of four churches from which in fourteenth century curfew was appointed to be rung – the others being St Mary-le-Bow, St Giles Cripplegate, and All Hallows, Barking.

[4] Similar to that under All Hallows, Barking.

137   St Bride, Fleet Street as restored 1957

Wren's altar-piece in Chapel Royal, Hampton Court, but with oval panel pierced and filled with incongruous stained glass. This erection hides most of the large east window above and around which is cunningly painted by Glyn Jones a Glory with angels and figures of Moses and Aaron[1] which it is hard to believe is a flat surface. He also designed the fine painting of the Crucifixion on the reredos and the glass panel above it. Over the return stalls are curious figures of 'Paul' and 'Bridget' by David McFall. The organ, although invisible, is unnecessarily powerful. Font cover is based on early design for St Bride's steeple.[2] Note in south-west corner of church figures of boy and girl from former school in Bride Lane. Fountain outside north door was gift of British Legion 1965 – John McCarthy, sculptor.

P.　ST CLEMENT EASTCHEAP, King William Street. Wren, 1683–87.

Ancient foundation, but first mention time of Henry III (1216–72). Of brick, with stone quoins, but stuccoed over. Interior, plain room with tapering south aisle, formerly with gallery over (destroyed by Butterfield 1872), now a chapel. He also rearranged the east end, divided reredos into three and altered east windows. Notice fine plaster wreath on ceiling. Organ by Renatus Harris. Note also the font (with Holy Dove in cover) beautiful pulpit, communion table (supported by four cherubs) and reredos (the latter reassembled and rendered splendid by the late Sir Ninian Comper, 1933) – also four doorcases of similar design (the east one with pediment) and fine Charles II Royal Arms on south wall, above carved bread-shelves and Benefaction tablets. Church redecorated 1968, with pillars and ceiling heavily coloured – the latter with much gold, to match Comper's work on reredos. Old Thomas Fuller, the church historian, was sometime lecturer here, as was also John Pearson, author of the Exposition of the Creed (died bishop of Chester, 1686).

ST DUNSTAN-IN-THE-EAST, Idol Lane, Eastcheap. Tower, Wren 1702; church rebuilt by Laing 1817–21.

Burnt out 1941. Temporary church under tower. Saxon dedication, but earliest reference 1250.

Partly burnt in 1666; Wren repaired church and built the famous steeple with spire poised on flying buttresses, similar in idea to that of St Nicholas, Newcastle, or St Giles, Edinburgh. Since the blitz this has been taken down and reconstructed. At base of tower note charming Gothic doorways and ironwork, also beauty of the weathering of the Portland stone, specially as seen in diffused evening light – jet black around doorways with their aureol of white crockets, bands of stripes immediately above, then brown and golden colours, leading to creamy white at summit. Plans were approved for St Dunstan to be a Church Information Centre, but through disagreements this was abandoned and the church is not to be rebuilt. But the walls have been preserved and, of course, the tower, with a tiny chapel constructed beneath it – also on N side, small room for meetings and, above, a flat for the rector of All Hallows, Barking, the priest in charge here. The churchyard (and walls of church, repaired with new window tracery) has been laid out as a garden by the Corporation. Until 1969 trees in churchyard included two planes (old), two limes, one laburnum, one peach, one fig and some privet bushes, with about 20 headstones around perimeter and some prostrate slabs.

G.　ST DUNSTAN-IN-THE-WEST, Fleet Street. Rebuilt 1831 by Shaw.

Damaged in the war, but repaired and reopened 1950. Earliest mention, 1237. Present church built back on old churchyard to widen street. Unusual octagonal plan, somewhat like St Bartholomew-the-Less, but with altar on north side and steeple on south. Latter very striking, its lantern being a close imitation of that of All Saints', Pavement at York, with flanking pinnacles added which improve design. Reredos largely made up of old foreign woodwork, more of which forms overmantle in vestry. Many fine monuments from the old church, tastefully disposed round walls, among which specially note brasses to Henry Dacres and his wife, 1530, and memorials to Cuthbert Fetherstone, the King's doorkeeper (bust in frame) 1615, Alex

---

[1] Deriving from an original feature of the church as described in *New View of London*, 1708.
[2] See Wren Society Vol IX, Plt. 9 (Reprod. p. 31).

138   Pre-War interior of St Dunstan-in-the-West

Layton 'ye famed swordsman', 1679. Damaris Turner, 1703, besides memorials to two Lord Mayors and other members of the Hoare family of banking fame, and donors of the reredos and window over it (now destroyed and replaced by new glass, 1950). Interior rearranged 1966 when the recess left of the altar was enclosed by elaborate nineteenth-century screen (Iconostasis) from the Autim Monastery, Bucharest for use on Sundays as a chapel by a Roumanian Orthodox congregation, St Dunstan's special concern being with Anglican relations with other churches abroad.

    Outside, notice statue of Queen Elizabeth

formerly on Ludgate (dem. 1760), also (in entrance to vestry), three other statues from the Gate – said to be of King Lud and his two sons and, inside door, an early nineteenth-century banner with view of the old church within a wreath of laurel. Note also clock with effigies which strike bells originally set up 1671 on old church, removed to St Dunstan, Regent's Park, 1831, and in 1935 returned to Fleet Street by first Viscount Rothermere, whose brother, Lord Northcliffe, is commemorated by outside monument designed by Sir Edwin Lutyens, P.R.A. Wm. Tyndale, translator of New Testament, preached here; the earl of Strafford, executed 1641, was here baptized; and Dr Thomas White, founder of Sion College (now on Embankment at Black-friars), was vicar (1623), followed by John Donne the distinguished but eccentric dean of St Paul's (d. 1631). Also, Izaak Walton, of piscatorial fame, was a parishioner and is commemorated by a stained glass window now hidden in Roumanian Chapel.

P. ST EDMUND, KING AND MARTYR, Lombard Street. Wren 1670–79; spire 1706–07.

St Edmund, king of East Anglia, was killed by Danes in 870. First mention time of Henry I (1100–35). As rebuilt, St Edmund stands north and south with altar at north end (as in St Dunstan West and St Botolph, Aldgate) but in this seems to have followed plan of old church – very unusual. Steeple has lead-covered, octagonal trumpet-shaped spire formerly adorned with 12 flaming urns. Note fine font (and rails) with four (out of 12) statues of apostles on cover, and richly carved pulpit; also, each side of entrance, churchwardens' pews, below a Lion and Unicorn on two of six carved pilasters of unknown origin or use, and on organ front, fine Stuart Royal Arms from St Dionis Backchurch (dem. 1878). On right-hand (east) wall note three panels (hatchments) of Royal Arms set up when church was put in mourning for Royal deaths.[1] These (from left to right) are for Princess Charlotte, (d. 1817), only child of Prince Regent, afterwards George IV, Edward duke of Kent (d. 1820) father of Queen Victoria and Royal Arms of 1816–37 (probably George IV). These came from All Hallows, Lombard Street.

St Edmund was restored by Rodney Tatchell in 1957, when metal was largely substituted for the old wooden roof and remains found of former semi-circular clerestory over altar.[2] Earlier, windows were repaired and new Royal Arms inserted in place of those of Queen Anne destroyed in raids. In 1968, church was redecorated under Mr Tatchell and eighteenth-century east vestry rebuilt and enlarged with upper storey.

G. ST ETHELBURGA, Bishopsgate. Pre-Fire. The dedication to Ethelburga, first abbess of Barking and daughter of Ethelbert, first Christian king of Kent, suggests ancient foundation, but earliest mention is 1250. Very small, but typical of the lesser pre-Fire City churches. Until about 1931, was entered beneath and between two tiny shops[3] with three large pairs of spectacles advertising their optician tenant. Vane on lantern has date 1671; formerly it surmounted a small spire. The interior, altered again and again in last 100 years, is not very interesting. The three pointed windows on each side have lost their tracery and the east window is Victorian, replacing a round-headed one like that still in south chapel. Note small organ high above western loft (1912) and the elaborate chancel screen (J.N. Comper, also 1912).

The mural over the altar, by Hans Feibusch (1963) shows the Crucified and Risen Christ centre, with St John and the Virgin below the Cross (left) and St Mary Magdalen on her knees with the Centurion behind (right). Above (left) is St Luke and a patient and (right) St Ethelburga talking to children. There is some fine seventeenth-century heraldic glass[4] and four striking stained glass windows by Leonard Walker. These commemorate the adventures of Henry Hudson, who, with 11 of his crew, received the Sacrament in this church before they left England in 1607 on their first voyage to discover the North-West Passage and the fourth is in memory of Dr Geikie-Cobb, rector 1900–1941. The nineteenth-century font has a Greek inscription, reading backwards and forwards. The cover (1686) is from St Swithun, Cannon Street, now demolished.

P.W. ST GILES CRIPPLEGATE. Pre-Fire, Victorian-ized.

Burnt out December 1940; now restored. Said to have been founded about 1090 by Alfune, a friend of Rahere (see St Bartholomew-the-Great), but this is disputed. Burnt 1545 and rebuilt.[5] Was a typical large pre-Fire City church, but had been

---

[1] There are other examples at St James Garlickhithe, St Magnus and St Mary-at-Hill.

[2] See volume of plans, elevations and sections of City churches in St Paul's Library.

[3] Built 1577 & 1615 (R. Com. Hist. Mons. Inventory of the City, p. 24).

[4] City of London and Mercers' Company (north side of chancel) and Saddlers' Company with Vintners' below (east window of chapel).

[5] In 1629 a crown of 5 pinnacles was erected on top of the tower after the fashion of old Bow church or Wren's St Dunstan-in-the-East. See 1633 edn. Stow's *Survey*.

139   St Ethelburga: engraving by West and Toms, 1736

refaced outside (except top of tower, altered 1683) and spruced up within. Many fine monuments; among those buried here were John Foxe, author of the *Book of Martyrs*, John Speed, the map publisher, Sir Martin Frobisher and John Milton and his father. Lancelot Andrews, one of the translators of the authorized version of the Bible, was vicar of St Giles 1588–1605. Oliver Cromwell was married here in 1620 and Milton was here reunited to his first wife, Mary Powell. Restored by Godfrey Allen who substituted a perpendicular east window for the former eighteenth-century oval one.[1] The lantern on the tower is a close copy of previous bell cage. Formerly there was a large churchyard with remains of two bastions of the City Wall (with a third just to the south) which were fully exposed by the raids. The church is now (1975) isolated among modern buildings and the churchyard replaced by a paved area with water on three sides.

To north of church a long lake with fountains on its further side connects along the west side with that on the south by the remains of the Roman Wall and corner bastion, the latter water suggesting the old City Ditch. At south-west corner of pavement, note seven rounded coffin-shaped tombstones, of early nineteenth-century date, which were dug up in the former churchyard. No doubt, they originally had head and foot stones, some of which may now be N side of church where 87 such stones, also from former graveyard, are set on top of a number of variously shaped brick structures about 18 inches high and several feet long. These are also intended for lunch-hour seats. Others on s side of church.

In St Giles a large organ loft was erected in 1969

----

[1] Before the blitz contained charming painted Glory with cherubs, dated 1792 [130].

140 St Ethelburga, *c.*1880

141 St Ethelburga after removal of shops and porch

to carry the reconstructed organ from St Luke[1] – note also fine font and cover in north-east corner, also from St Luke. No monuments survive beyond two busts on north and south walls (Sir W. Staines and John Milton) and some fragments of sixteenth- and seventeenth-century monuments on sill of west window of south aisle. The other tablets are from St Luke.

At west end, note busts of Milton, Bunyan, Defoe and Cromwell, on loan from the Cripplegate Institute – Milton's statue was formerly outside.

P. ST HELEN, BISHOPGATE. Pre-Fire.
Maybe of Saxon foundation, but first mention is mid-twelfth century. In 1212 a Benedictine nunnery was established in St Helen which hereafter was used jointly by the nuns and the parishioners, between whom was a screen; and dual usage is shown by the church's unusual structure – two naves separated by a single arcade, the lofty western arches dating from 1475. The northern nave was the nuns', the southern the parishioners'. There is a south transept and between the two naves a small seventeenth-century western turret of wood continued internally down to the floor. In the south wall is a beautiful doorway dated 1633 with contemporary doors. The interior (still dark with Victorian stained glass, but partially lightened by clearance of three windows on south side, 1969) is full of interest, containing a combined 'Easter Sepulchre' 'squint' for the nuns, and tomb, 13 of the nuns' stalls, a fine Jacobean pulpit, two handsome inner doorcases,[2] a simple but elegant font and the earliest sword-rest in the City – of wood dated 1665; also, by south porch, original altar-

[1] Old Street.
[2] The westernmost with the inscription 'This is none other than the House of God, this is the Gate of Heaven'.

table from St Martin Outwich (dem. 1874) and high up on the north side, two windows of old heraldic glass. There are seven brasses and a long series of monuments of exceptional interest. They include tombs to John Oteswich and wife, with effigies, late fourteenth-century, brought from St Martin; Sir John Crosby and wife, with effigies, 1476 (he built Crosby Place, the hall of which, pulled down in 1908, is now re-erected at Chelsea); Sir Julius Caesar (Adelmare), Master of the Rolls, in marble in the form of a sealed document; Sir Thomas Gresham, founder of the Royal Exchange and of Gresham College, and Sir John Spencer, 1609, newly coloured and gilt, besides many other very fine Elizabethan and later monuments. Fine rectory and offices (s.w. corner) erected 1968. The potential value of lunch-hour services in the City is demonstrated at St Helen by packed congregations of young businessmen on Tuesdays and Thursdays.

P.   ST JAMES GARLICKHITHE, Upper Thames Street. Wren, 1674–87.

Damaged in last war and long under repair. Steeple 1714–17. First mention *c.*1170. Stow says so called because 'of old time on the banke of . . . Thames near this church Garlicke was usually solde'. The tower, lately new-faced, is surmounted by a charming steeple generally similar to those of St Michael Royal and St Stephen Walbrook, but all three have notable differences. Until the blitz, the tower carried a projecting clock, with figure of St James. Interior unusual in arrangement: six columns forming narrow aisle on each side, broken in centre to form shallow internal transepts. Recess for altar. In porch under tower note two tablets recording rebuilding of church under Wren, and nineteenth-century restorations and, in west gallery, fine organ by Father Smith in splendid case, also attractive ironwork (hat stands, etc) on churchwardens' pews and elsewhere; holy table richly carved with scrolls, doves and cherub-heads, two sets of Lion and Unicorn, one from St Michael Queenhithe (dem. 1876), which also provided the fine pulpit, and carved Stuart Royal Arms in vestibule. At St James, before the war, were four Royal Hatchments for George III, William IV, Princess Charlotte, and, perhaps, George IV[1] – only

two remain.[2] In a cupboard is preserved a mummified body – dubbed 'Jimmy Garlick', identity unknown – found many years ago in vault. A service here in 1711 is described by Steele in *The Spectator*, No. 147 (18 August 1711). Repair of church under Lockhart Smith had many setbacks, but was at last completed and St James rehallowed, 3 October 1963. The gateway from Garlic Hill with vine motive was given by Vintners' Company, while the glass chandelier in the nave was given by the Glass Sellers' Company. The reredos has been handsomely decorated with Commandments, Creed and Lord's Prayer, restored in place of intruded Victorian pictures, while large painting of the Ascension by Andrew Geddes, A.R.A., given in 1815, has been cleaned at expense of the Painter-Stainers' Company. Church now exposed by widening of Thames Street.

G.   ST KATHERINE CREECHURCH, Leadenhall Street. Pre-Fire.

Creechurch is a corruption of Christchurch, derived from being in the churchyard of the great Priory of Holy Trinity, often called Christchurch, founded by Maud, Queen of Henry I, in 1108. Apparently built early in the thirteenth century. The tower dates from 1504, but the rest of the church was rebuilt 1628–31 and consecrated by Laud, with many 'advanced' ceremonies. It shows a curious mixture of styles, the exterior originally having a bizarre cresting to the walls (one item remains beside the west window) while within, the Classical pillars and arches contrast strangely with the shouldered Gothic windows and 'vaulted' plaster ceiling, with bosses of the City Arms and those of the chief City Companies. The effect is very picturesque. Note the east window with Catherine wheel upper part, containing old glass, the lower previously displayed the Royal Arms. Also fine Adam period communion table and earlier doorway to vestry. Font has arms of Sir John Gayer, Lord Mayor in 1646 – an annual sermon is preached here to commemorate his escape from a lion. The most noteworthy monument is in south aisle – to Sir Nicholas Throckmorton (d. 1571), sometime ambassador to France and Chief Butler of England.

---

[1] See St Edmund King and Martyr.

[2] Not now on show, but two private hatchments adorn s. wall.

142   St Katherine Cree: West and Toms' engraving of 1736 before 18th-century alterations to the tower doorway, removal of the curious parapet crestings and renewal of the turret

143   St Katherine Cree, looking north-east

Throgmorton Street is named after him, Curious gateway with skeleton, formerly next the east end, now faces churchyard (invisible from street) which has two large plane trees. Note large sundial on south front of church with motto: *Non sine lumine*. The date MDCCVI (1706) formerly there, is now gone. Circular turret on tower replaced an older turret in the eighteenth century. Although little damaged in the war, St Katherine's was long neglected and was closed as a dangerous structure. In examining roof, much of the ceiling was regrettably destroyed, but the church was at last restored under Marshall Sisson following urgent appeals from Royal Fine Art Commission and Central Council for the Care of Churches and was reopened as the H.Q. of the Industrial Christian Fellowship on 6 July 1962 with offices in the aisles against which are devices of organizations connected with the Fellowship. At east end of the aisle is a Laud Memorial Chapel of 'Blessed King Charles the Martyr', dedicated by Bishop Wand, 1962.

G.   ST LAWRENCE JEWRY, Gresham Street. Wren 1670–87.
Burnt out December, 1940. Temporary church under tower until rebuilding. Called Jewry from Jews living hereabouts before their expulsion from England in 1290. The great-grandfather of Anne Boleyn and the father of Sir Thomas Gresham (see St Helen) were buried in the old church. Present church one of the largest and most expensive rebuilt by Wren (cost £11,870) and the east front the most Classical of his compositions. Its tower sustained a lead-covered spire, topped by a vane in form of gridiron emblem of its patron saint which was saved and has been replaced on a replica of the old steeple. Interior was noted for magnificent woodwork, etc, especially the organ case, doorcases and vestry panelling, etc, now alas destroyed, one of the greatest losses of the war. St Lawrence was restored by Cecil Brown and opened 17 July 1957. It is sumptuously furnished with much gold, largely at the expense of the City Corporation, whose special church it is. All the fittings are new, the furniture of a curiously impervious looking dark polished wood. The organ in the west gallery recalls the former splendid instrument. Note the brass chandeliers and wooden

screen between nave and wide north aisle, which has Commonwealth Chapel at east end and is closed on west for vestries with vicarage above. All the windows are filled with stained glass by Christopher Webb, which although very un-Wrenlike is carefully designed, reminiscent of the late Sir Ninian Comper – note especially the 'Wren and craftsmen' window in the vestibule with its delicate City steeples.

The askew and asymmetrical west end, never meant to be seen, was opened up by demolitions.

P.   ST MAGNUS, Lower Thames Street. Wren, 1671–87; steeple 1703–06.
Damaged in last war, restored 1951. Dedication rare. This Magnus must have been an earlier saint than Magnus of Orkney who was only canonized in 1135, as the church was in existence at time of William I (1066–87). Stood at head of Old London Bridge, the footway to which passed under the tower after the houses on the bridge were demolished in 1760 when west ends of aisles were taken down, thus spoiling symmetry of front to Thames Street. Steeple one of Wren's most complex and striking erections, but is shamefully hidden by Adelaide House. The fine projecting clock is dated 1709, but appears to be earlier; it was formerly embellished with emblematical statues and was the gift of Sir Charles Duncombe, Lord Mayor, who also gave the handsome organ[1]. Interior contains western vestibule beneath organ gallery, magnificent reredos (partly modern), reredos to south altar incorporating former south doorcase, carved pulpit with splendid tester (cf St Stephen Walbrook) and handsome font, near which note large benefactors' board in carved frame with painting of Charity in cartouche at top. Also fine sword-rest on pillar, dated 1708, but painted with Royal Arms of 1800–1816, while in the vestibule are three Royal Hatchments[2] for (from north to south) George III's Queen Charlotte, d. 1818, Princess Charlotte, daughter of Prince Regent, died 1817, and George IV's Queen Caroline, d. 1821.

In westernmost window of north side, note made-

---

[1] By Abraham Jordan, 1712; contained first example of 'swell' organ.
[2] See St Edmund King and Martyr.

up panel of old glass with arms of City of London and the Plumbers' Company – from their former Hall. Four windows on south side by Lawrence Lee, the heraldic windows on north side by Alfred L. Wilkinson. Now circular, these windows were made so in 1782 to keep out noise. Henry Yevele (d. 1400), architect to Edward III, Richard II and Henry IV, was buried in the old church and Miles Coverdale, publisher of first complete English Bible (1535), was rector here 1564–6. Since 1920, St Magnus has been representative of the extreme Anglo-Catholic tradition. The church was re-decorated in 1965.

P.W. ST MARGARET, LOTHBURY, behind Bank of England. Wren, 1686–93; steeple 1698–1700.
The meaning of 'Lothbury' is uncertain. First mention of St Margaret is about 1200. Present church formerly had small shops against front. Note elegant steeple. Interior contains much old furniture, some of it from other churches, especially fine screen[1] and sounding-board to pulpit from All Hallows, Thames Street (dem. 1894) – the pulpit is St Margaret's and All Hallows' pulpit is at St Paul's, Hammersmith. Organ from St Olave Old Jewry, (dem. 1888) in proper place on west gallery. Reredos, spoilt by incongruous paintings, is now restored with Decalogue, Creed and Lord's Prayer, by Rodney Tatchell.[2] The chapel in south aisle dates from 1891 – its reredos came from St Olave and its screen (dated), designed by G.F. Bodley incorporatates altar-rails from same church (lower part). In this chapel, note charming font on black and white marble step sculptured with appropriate Biblical subjects – Adam and Eve, Noah's Ark, Baptism of Christ and Baptism of the Eunuch. Also two busts at west end of Mrs Simpson, by Nollekens, 1795 and of the great engraver and publisher, Alderman Boydell, Lord Mayor, 1790, designed by Banks, also from St Olave, while in north-west corner of church is fine bronze bust of Sir Peter Le Maire (d. 1631) by Hubert Le Sueur, from St Christopher-le-Stocks (dem. 1781). Until 1954, St Margaret served six parishes besides its own, due to union of adjacent parishes and demolition of their churches; and this accounts for the large number of memorials on the walls. The tower and south front were washed 1969. There is a small

court behind church, originally the graveyard. This is mostly paved, but contains a plane tree and, against old house on west side,[3] two tall fig trees. Note fountain.

G. ST MARGARET PATTENS, Eastcheap. Wren, 1684–89; steeple 1689–1701.
Stow says so called because old-time pattens (iron clogs worn to keep shoes out of mud) were sold nearby, but the earlier references indicate that it refers to a benefactor named Patynz or Patins. The beautiful but simple spire of Wren's church is said to be 199 ft. high – his third highest. Six circular windows on west front. Inside note west gallery carrying organ, canopied churchwardens' pews before it,[4] Royal Arms (Charles II), graceful font and fine carving on reredos. Also Lion and Unicorn at entrance to chancel, two sword-rests, beadle's pew in north-east corner, two late eighteenth-century needlework panels in south-east corner and interesting old views of church in vestibule. St Margaret was restored in 1955–6, when gallery in north aisle was closed in, as is east end of the aisle below, with a chapel to the west. In south alley is a floor slab (1686) to James Donaldson, of the Weavers' Company, 'City Garbler'. This official, of ancient standing, was inspector of drugs, spices, etc. Note also two charming Wren-period monuments on piers of north aisle. Thomas Birch, D.D., F.R.S., rector 1746–1766, was secretary of the Royal Society and a prolific writer. The church is now a Christian Study Centre.

G. ST MARTIN, Ludgate Hill. Wren, 1677–87. First mention 1174.
Adjoined Ludgate (dem. 1780) and remains of City wall still against west wall of church and beyond it.

---

[1] One of only two screens erected in Wren's churches – the other being at St Peter, Cornhill. Splendid Stuart Royal Arms, formerly double-faced and over centre of All Hallows' screen, removed years ago and divided, one face being given away. Remaining face replaced on screen 1969.

[2] A large and elaborate, but inappropriate, stone carving of the Ascension was erected over the altar in 1910, designed by son of the then rector, Preb. Ingram; it is now covered up. Paintings of Moses and Aaron on east wall come from St Christopher-le-Stocks.

[3] Alas, demolished 1971!

[4] On one of these 'C.W.' is pointed out as standing for 'Christopher Wren', but it can equally mean 'churchwarden'.

Wren kept St Martin's quiet from traffic noises by placing tower symmetrically in south front and within forming centre of lofty aisle which opens to the church by three splendid coffered arches. These are closed below to form vestibules which supported galleries now gone. Note three beautiful doorcases, and another, opposite. Interior very lofty with tall pillars forming internal cruciform arrangement as at St Anne and St Agnes, but proportions being dissimilar, the effect is different. Organ properly placed in west gallery beneath which note font with Greek inscription which reads both ways (see St Ethelburga), and white marble Pelican in its Piety (see St Mary Abchurch and St Michael, Cornhill). Fine reredos, pulpit and remarkable double chair in chancel. Also central chandelier, and, high on south wall, Royal Arms, Stuart, but shield repainted with present Arms. Also possesses fine carved bread-shelves (see also St Clement Eastcheap and St Peter, Cornhill). Note also bell of 1693 on square iron chest in north-east corner of church and embossed coffin plate of Daniel Pinder, 1820, on north wall.

In 1886 the Wren church of St Mary Magdalen, Knightrider Street was burnt down and later demolished, the parish being united to St Martin. Among several items removed to the latter church, note, in vestry, a small brass plate dated 1586 and rescued from the Great Fire of 1666, with figure in fur gown (said to be Thos. Beri, or Berry) and lines of various hortative themes, ending with a benefaction of 12 loaves to as many poor people per week.

Also on east wall, north of the altar, is a large painting of Our Lord's Ascension by R. Browne, 1720.[1] The panels on east wall, south of altar are copies by 'a modern Belgian artist'[2] of St Mary Magdalen, St Gregory and St Martin. Interior is beautifully kept.

Without, notice quiet beauty of front with lovely scrolled trusses leading up to massive tower and elegant lead-covered spire which contrasts so effectively with St Paul's mighty dome. The vicar's special subject – liaison with Police.

G. ST MARY ABCHURCH, Cannon Street. Wren, 1681–87.

Damaged but now restored. Temporary church was in rectory room, adjoining church. The meaning of the prefix Ab (earlier Abbe) is not certainly known – possibly it commemorates a founder or benefactor named Abba or Abbo. First mention, twelfth century. Badly damaged in 1940, when painted dome was nearly destroyed. This painting, unique in a City church, was by William Snow, painter-stainer and carver, and has been beautifully restored by Walter Hoyle. Its chief features are a Glory within a choir of angels, and, below, 8 symbolic figures of Christian Virtues. There is much fine furniture, especially splendid doorcases (cf St Martin, Ludgate); pulpit and tester (cf All Hallows, Lombard Street, now at Twickenham); font with figures of the four Evangelists on cover, under a beautiful west gallery, which carries new organ with front from All Hallows, Bread Street (dem. 1878); handsome altar-table, with carved scrolls beneath and magnificent reredos. This, perhaps the finest in the City, is known to be by Grinling Gibbons himself, for documents proving this, including a letter in Gibbons' own hand, were discovered in 1946 in a church chest.

Note also original carved pews against north, south and west walls (the quantity of pierced and other carving round church is astonishing), Royal Arms (Stuart) over south doorcase, Lion and Unicorn on front pews, two sword-rests and a Poor Box by entrance. There is a handsome monument to Sir Patience Ward, Lord Mayor, 1680 and many other very fine memorials on north and south walls. The exterior of church – brick, with stone quoins – was formerly stuccoed over. Note paving of geometrical design on site of churchyard. Beneath this in 1940, a result of a raid, was discovered a crypt, probably fourteenth-century, besides another of later date, under the church. Over the north doorway is a pelican and nest in copper,[3] originally the vane of the spire, which

---

[1] Often erroneously attributed to Benjamin West.

[2] Philip Norman, in St Paul's Ecclesiological Society, Vol VI (1909).

[3] Known in heraldry as a Pelican in its Piety, being a well-known symbol for the Eucharist. (Cf. Pelican on the altarpiece feeding its young with its own blood.)

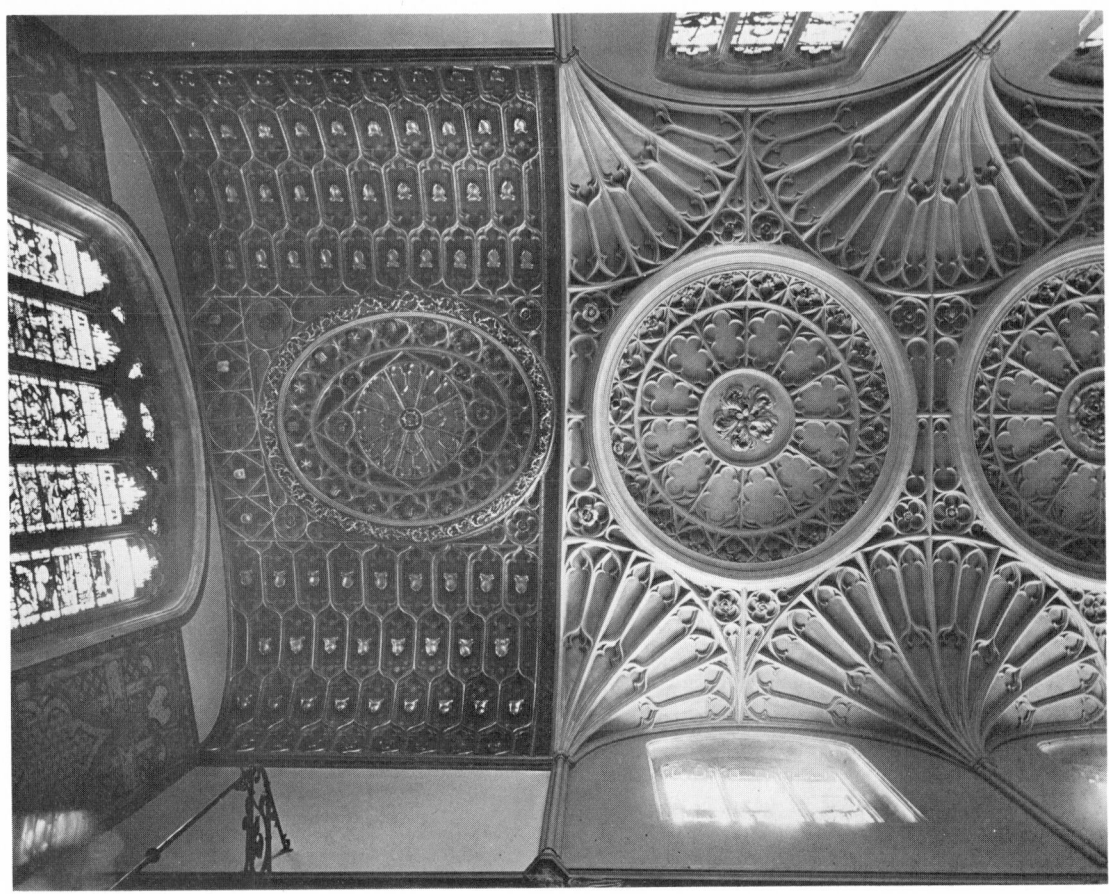

144   St Mary Aldermary: ceiling of nave and sanctuary, showing askew east wall

cost £80. This was displaced in 1764 for an ordinary flag vane, now itself gone, since the upper part of the spire was rebuilt in 1884. St Mary has been finely restored by Godfrey Allen and its interior is perhaps now the least altered of any of Wren's churches.

ST MARY, ALDERMANBURY
Foundations still remain *in situ*, but church now removed to Fulton, Missouri. See page 172.

ST MARY ALDERMARY, Queen Victoria Street. Wren's Gothic, Victorianized.
Church opened 1682. Tower (upper part) 1701–04. Stow says named Aldermary 'because the same was very old and elder than any church of St Marie in the Citie'. If this is correct, the church must date

from a remote period, but the meaning seems uncertain. First mention about 1080. Rebuilt by Henry Keeble, Lord Mayor, 1511, but tower unfinished at his death and remained so until 1629, when it was completed by legacies from Wm. Rodoway and Richard Pierson.[1] Tower not destroyed in Great Fire and repaired by Wren who rebuilt upper part and designed church in Gothic style[2] with remarkable fan-vaulted ceiling. One Henry Rogers left £5,000 towards the cost. The fittings

---

[1] The panelling of the corner turrets of this tower, unlike any other in England (?) is identical with that shown on a fifteenth-century drawing of a tower (never built) for King's College, Cambridge (in British Museum). See plt, Lysar's *Cambs*, 1808.
[2] Severely plain outside, the present buttresses and east end pinnacles being Victorian. Exterior (except upper part of tower) cleaned, 1969, and decayed surfaces renewed.

were Classical and were mostly replaced by 'correct' Gothic furniture in 1876–77, but the west door-case, font (dated 1682), pulpit and very fine wooden sword-rest (also dated 1682) were allowed to remain.

The tower pinnacles originally ended in balls and vanes, which were displaced in the later eighteenth century by slender stone finials. These were clumsily renewed in 1876 and finally taken down about 1927. New finials in fibre-glass, gilded, were erected May 1962, close copies of the pre-1876 ones. The interior, blasted in air raids, has been restored. New windows by Messrs Lee & Crawford, including fine heraldry (Keeble, Rogers and City Companies). Here John Milton married his third wife, Elizabeth Minshall, 1663.[1]

P.W. ST MARY-AT-HILL, Lovat Lane, Eastcheap. Wren, 1670–76 and later.

First mention 1177, and from that time until the Reformation, the town house of the abbots of Waltham was situated on the south side of St Mary: so close was it that permission had to be obtained to demolish the kitchen when the parishioners wanted to extend the south aisle of their church (part of a general rebuilding) at the end of the fifteenth century. Only partly destroyed in the Great Fire, and repaired by Wren, who rebuilt east end and interior, but old west end and tower remained till 1787–88, and side walls until 1826–7 when they were respectively rebuilt. Has internal cruciform arrangement as at St Anne and St Agnes and St Martin, Ludgate, but with shallow dome in centre. The details of ceiling of later date than Wren, having been renewed 1826 in Adam style by Savage. The old pews (only ones left in City), organ case (Father Smith), font and reredos remain, but the pulpit (either wholly or in part), the reading desk and carvings on gallery-front were produced 1848–50 by W. Gibbs Rogers and are so very like work of Wren's time as to be hardly distinguishable from it. Rogers also worked at St Michael, Cornhill. Note fine Stuart Royal Arms and four hatchments for George IV, Queen Adelaide, Duchess of Kent (mother of Queen Victoria) and Prince Consort.[2] Note also Resurrection stone in vestibule (see St Andrew, Holborn) and fine projecting clock at east end; also entrance, with skull and bones,

to quaint passage beneath the old rectory, leading to Lovat Lane. Churchyard on north side, laid out as garden of rest. Stow says Thomas Beckett was parson of St Mary. Edward Young, author of *Night Thoughts*, was married here, 1731, and Rev. Thos. Brand, author of *Popular Antiquities* (pub. 1772), was rector here and Secretary of the Society of Antiquaries, while at the end of last century St Mary was made famous by the evangelistic work of its rector, Rev. (later Preb.) Wilson Carlile, and of the Church Army, which he founded. Interior redecorated 1968 when ceiling and splendid reredos received much gilding and heraldic roundels were inserted in east windows.[3]

P. ST MARY-LE-BOW, OR BOW CHURCH, Cheapside. Wren, 1670–83.

Burnt out 1941. Of very ancient foundation – first mention *c.*1090. Name derived from the 'bows' or arches of the early Norman crypt beneath the church which also gave name to the Court of Arches, formerly and now again held here. This crypt, of about 1090, was the basement of what was, apparently, one of the earliest stone churches in London. Before the war it consisted of a nave with brick vault (mostly of Wren's time) supported by monolith columns with cushion capitals and two aisles with ancient vaulting, the southern walled up. This has now been opened and fitted up as a chapel, consecrated 24 February 1960, and this and the nave (used as Court of Arches) have received new (concrete) vaults. The northern aisle, entirely rebuilt, is now used for secular purposes.

In the early sixteenth century the tower of the old church was crowned with five lanterns, four at the angles and one held aloft on flying buttresses. (Compare Wren's St Dunstan-in-the-East steeple.) St Mary was always of great importance (in the fourteenth century it was one of the four City

---

[1] At St Mary were held St Antholin's Lectures (established 1559 at nearby church of St Antholin (dem. 1875) at a service each day, Monday–Friday, 1.15 to 2 o'clock). Since the war reduced in number – one always to be held at St Mary and one at two or three other City churches at the discretion of the trustees.

[2] See St Edmund King and Martyr.

[3] These roundels and inscriptions came from big north and south windows, where the roundels took the place, after the last war, of original dark Victorian glass, within the still existing borders.

145   St Mary-le-Bow as restored 1964

churches appointed to ring the curfew – see St Bride), but the tower stood back from Cheapside. Wren emphasized the church's importance by bringing his tower forward to the street and by giving it his most elaborate and beautiful spire. In view of its early date, this is striking proof of his early maturity as an architect. The steeple was badly calcined in the raids and its remarkable wooden spiral staircase destroyed[1]. The spire proper was taken down, reconstructed and the bells reinstated and rung by H.R.H. Prince Philip on 20 December 1961. Notice beautiful corner ornaments at base of spire (a close copy of those flanking the dome in an early engraving of the Sorbonne, Paris – Seckler, p. 104) and the vane – a flying dragon eight or nine feet long. In the two tower

doorways Wren has given us perhaps the finest Classical entrances in England. The interior of the church had been spoilt by tasteless alterations. After the raids a temporary church was built on site of vestry, and the arcades of the church, seemingly intact were later demolished. After long delays St Mary was finished under direction of Laurence King, and rehallowed 11 June 1964 with spacious sanctuary for free-standing altar, with bishop's chair behind, and large pendent rood with figures of St Mary and St John, St Mary Magdalen and the Centurion. This rood, the stained glass windows, and the etched glass screen in the crypt, were

---

[1] This was centrally supported in, but did not touch, the 9-in. thick wall of the brick cylinder carrying the upper colonnade.

designed by John Hayward, the organ on west gallery made by Rushworth and Dreaper and the case and vestibule doorcase by Dove Brothers. The greenish woodwork of the eastern part of the church was by Faithcraft and the metal screens by Grundy Arnatt. There is no permanent seating, chairs being brought in for services. The rector's lodgings are above the vestibule and sacristy (vestry). Crowded congregations witness the popularity of the Tuesday lunchtime 'dialogues' between notable people and the rector.

G. ST MARY WOOLNOTH, Lombard Street. Hawksmoor, 1716–27.

Probably pre-Conquest in origin, but first mention end of twelfth century. Woolnoth seems to be derived from someone called Wulfnoth. Only damaged in the Great Fire and repaired by Wren, but had to be pulled down 1716.[1] Nicholas Hawksmoor, the most individual of Wren's pupils, built six London churches – of these, St Mary is perhaps the most original and has one of the finest sites in the City (formerly it was almost hidden by houses). It shows the architect at his best; the west front, with strong oblong tower and square turrets and fine entrance, and north side, with elaborate and beautiful niches, make the exterior one of the most striking in London. The interior is perhaps unique with cube-like proportions and clusters of great Corinthian columns. The fittings, in spite of re-arrangement in 1876, are notable, especially the fine reredos (in form of baldacchino), curiously shaped pulpit, and beautiful iron altar-rails. Note also handsome fronts of former galleries now against the walls. In 1897–1900 the Bank station was constructed beneath the church and cherubs carved on side doorways of front look out as one descends to the trains. John Newton, the evangelist, was rector here 1779–1807 – his epitaph, written by himself, is on north wall. In chancel are buried ashes of St Mary's last rector, Prebendary Wm. Holland (1933–51), inscribed 'He walked with God'. Between the pulpit and north wall is a corner for the Association of Men of Kent and Kentish Men. The church was re-decorated in 1968, when the reredos was relettered (on new boards over the old), new Royal Arms were inserted beneath the east clerestory window and the exterior cleaned.

P. ST MICHAEL, CORNHILL. Wren, 1670–77, Victorianized. (Tower, Hawksmoor.)

One of the few Saxon foundations in the City, it being given about 1055 to the Abbey of Evesham by Alnothus or Alnod, the priest. The mediaeval church had many chantries and fraternities and in the fifteenth century was fully pewed, men and women being segregated. St Michael seems always to have had a prominent tower, which was spired before 1421[2] when it was rebuilt. This second tower survived the Great Fire and was patched up by Wren when he rebuilt the church in his usual Classical style. In 1715 the old steeple had become unsafe and was eventually rebuilt in the Gothic manner by Hawksmoor. It is a grand tower with elaborately carved pinnacles – note sculptured heads, young and old, three-quarters of the way up. Often said to be modelled on Magdalen Tower, Oxford, but there is little resemblance. Interior of church remodelled by Sir G.G. Scott, 1857–60, who inserted 'Venetian' tracery in windows (which were filled with rich, dark stained glass) and added excessively ornamented north porch of exotic design. About 1950 the windows were lightened by substituting plain glass for the dark backgrounds, and the clever carvings of flowers, etc, on the bench-ends, by W. Gibbs Rogers (see St Mary-at-Hill) can now be seen without artificial light. Note carved pelican of 1775, formerly on the reredos, almost sole survivor of the old fittings.[3] Fabyan the chronicler was buried here and in the present church there are several monuments to members of the Cowper family. The churchyard remains on south side of church. In sixteenth century it contained a preaching cross[4] and was surrounded by a cloister, in the garth of which were buried the father, grandfather and great-grandfather of John Stow (see St Andrew Undershaft). The grandfather in his will, 1527, directed his 'body to be buryed in the litell

[1] Two reclining effigies and a floor slab to members of the Viner family from the old church, now in Gautby Church, Lincs.

[2] See pen-drawing in Great Book of Accounts beginning 1456.

[3] The font bowl is also old, dated 1672.

[4] Built by Sir John Rudstone, Lord Mayor, 1528.

grene Churchyard of the Parysshe Church of Seynt Myghel in Cornhyll, between the Crosse and the Church Wall . . . by my Father and Mother, Systers and Brothers, and also my own Childerne'. The church was newly decorated in 1969.

W. ST MICHAEL PATERNOSTER ROYAL. Wren, 1686–94; steeple 1715–17.

Shattered by flying bombs in July 1944. First mention 1219. One part of name derived from former nearby Paternoster Lane, probably so called from Paternoster or rosary makers. Royal comes from connection of neighbouring wine-trade district (Vintry Ward) with the town of La Réole, near Bordeaux. Tower Royal, a small street close by, recalled a fourteenth-century mansion also so named. The famous Dick Whittington, four times Mayor of London, rebuilt St Michael and established a college therein (hence College Hill) in 1423 and was here buried. The charming stone steeple crowning the tower of Wren's church is octagonal in plan, but otherwise recalls those of St James Garlickhithe and St Stephen Walbrook. The fine reredos and pulpit and other fittings were fortunately removed to safety before the church was blasted by the two flying bombs which brought down the roof, etc. The vestry at the east end had an elaborate plaster cornice with heraldic and other devices, now mostly destroyed. After first-aid repairs, St Michael was open for a time, but was closed about 1955, and after long neglect has now been restored by Elidir Davies as a dual purpose building. St Michael was rehallowed on 19 December 1968, in presence of H.R.H. The Duke of Edinburgh as Headquarters of the Missions to Seamen. All woodwork, whether old or new, of a greenish oak colour (except the organ). The reredos and pulpit, deteriorated since the war, have been beautifully restored. Note also splendid three-tier candelabrum and graceful figure of Charity (now adorning the modern lectern) both from All Hallows-the-Great (demolished 1894) as also figures of Moses and Aaron on the east wall (from All Hallows' reredos). Three east windows, formerly walled up, now contain stained glass by John Hayward, representing, centre, St Michael overthrowing Satan, left, St Mary holding aloft the Christ child who is spearing a seven-headed dragon

and, right, St Gabriel with Adam and Eve and the Serpent. The west window on south side (also by Hayward) is remarkable in representing Dick Whittington (with his cat) so garbed as to suggest Sherlock Holmes or a gamekeeper!

Following recent legislation St Michael has been deprived of its Guild status and is now a chapel under the jurisdiction of the bishop of London.

ST. MILDRED, BREAD STREET, Cannon Street. Wren, 1681–87.

Destroyed by bombs, April and May 1941. First mention 1170, when one Richard was priest. The old church had stone spire struck by lightning, 1559. The Royalist, Sir Nicholas Crispe, gave an elaborate east window in 1629; he was buried here 1665. Above the late church he was commemorated by the weathervane of the lead-covered spire, which showed the Crispe arms and a monogram of M.B. Wren gave this small oblong church a most charming interior with shallow dome on arches. Escaping 'restoration', it retained the old pews, splendid pulpit, reredos, Royal Arms, etc, up to its destruction in 1941. The fittings were being bricked up for safety, but just too late – most of them perished. The loss of this interior was one of the heaviest in the war. The brick tower, almost the sole remains of the church, was formerly invisible from the street. The poet Shelley was here married to Mary Wollstonecraft, 1816. In 1932, elaborate exterior bronze memorial to Adm. Arthur Phillip, founder of Australia, who was born in Bread Street Ward, was placed on front of St Mildred – the gift of the late Lord Wakefield. The bust and plates from this memorial were erected on Gateway House (north side of Cannon Street), 1968. The site is now built over.

G. ST NICHOLAS COLE ABBEY, Queen Victoria Street. Wren, 1671–81.

Burnt out May, 1941. Restored 1962. First mention, 1241–59 and all early references have 'Cold Abbey' which seems to be corruption of Cold Harbour (a shelter for travellers, a 'cold shelter'), which, as a name, occurs many times in various parts of the country. In London, besides a former royal mansion in Thames Street, it is found (either now or previously), in The Tower, in Camberwell and Clerkenwell and there was a Cold Abbey in St Sepulchre's parish in 1361. Before Queen Victoria Street was made (1867–71) entrance was on north side in Knightrider Street, and up to about 50 years ago the south side was over a vent of the underground railway (later built over) and the smoke from the then steam trains so blackened it that the church was nicknamed St Nicholas Cole Hole Abbey! The tower was surmounted by a curious octagonal trumpet-shaped spire with ball and delicate vane. (Compare St Edmund, Lombard Street.) The church has now been drastically restored by Arthur Bailey, especially the tower, the upper half of which was taken down and re-built with a new spire, a little higher than before. Rehallowed 10 May 1962. The vane is an old one, being the fine model of a ship from St Michael Queenhithe (dem. 1876) and from then until 1962 on a spirelet on the site in Thames Street. The Victorian windows of the south front, formerly built against, are now opened up and glazed and the three east windows filled with rich stained glass by Keith New. They are said to represent: centre, 'the Rock of Christ' with the ark (the church) with four rivers (the Gospels) spreading to the side windows; left, St Nicholas Cole Abbey in centre of the globe with crosses pointing to four corners of the world; right, seven lamps (gifts of the Holy Spirit), the whole to represent the extension of the Church overseas. The pulpit and font cover are old as also are six carved panels from the west screen, now reinstated, and carvings from the former reredos now over the south doorway. Behind panelling near this door is set a mediaeval stone head found during the restoration.

P. ST OLAVE, HART STREET, Fenchurch Street. Pre-Fire.
Blasted and burnt April and May, 1941. Restored 1954. Dedicated to Olaf, king of Norway, martyred 1030. Earliest mention, time of Henry I (1100–1135). Was typical of smaller mediaeval City churches. Tower heightened with brick and turret added 1732. After wrecking of church, Sunday worship was held in St Edmund, Lombard Street, until end of 1947, when for three months congregation squeezed into tiny late Norman crypt in All Hallows Staining churchyard, corner of Mark Lane and Fenchurch Street. This crypt, placed here in 1873, was a relic of the old Hermitage of St James-on-the-Wall, Monkwell Street, near Cripplegate, removed 1872 on demolition of Lamb's Chapel built over it. Then from 1948 to 1954 worship was carried on in a temporary church built against tower of All Hallows Staining (church dem. 1870) which faced west instead of east so as to use tower as chancel. This church is now removed and a church hall, gift of the Cloth-workers' Company, built alongside the site. St Olave was restored by the late Ernest Glanfield 1951–54, King Haakon VII of Norway and the bishop of London laying dedication stones. Re-hallowed 9 April 1954. Tower has received new bell turret larger than before and a porch has been built against the old south door. The arcades are largely intact and the pulpit, from St Benet Grace-church (dem. 1867), now beautifully cleaned, and fine altar-rails with little couchant lions removed for safety, survive; new organ is concealed by a western screen. The charming font replaces a Victorian one. Note four fine sword-rests, between nave and chancel. The three east windows by A.E. Buss, 1953, represent, centre, Christ Crucified and Reigning, with St Olave, north and St George, south; left, The Virgin and Child between Queen Elizabeth I with bells of All Hallows Staining and St Catherine for St Katherine Coleman (dem. 1926) with above, small figures of Elizabeth Fry, Florence Nightingale, Josephine Butler, and Edith Cavell, right, St Clement, with arms of Trinity House, left, and H.R.H. The Duke of Gloucester, right. A.E. Buss also designed the Arms, in aisle windows, of Port of London Authority (north) and Cloth-workers' Company (south). Note also over south door, memorial window to Viscount Monsell of Evesham, with good heraldry, by John Hayward. The only pre-war glass is the Churchwardens' (Armorial) window,[1] nineteenth and twentieth centuries. There were many fine brasses and monu-ments (see Povah's Annals of St Olave, Hart Street – copy in church), some of which have been saved. Note Riccard statue, 1672 (north aisle), the Bayning monument, 1616 (north side of sanctuary), and fine Jacobean Deane Memorial, 1608 (over vestry

---

[1] In north aisle.

146   St Olave, Hart Street, in 1837 from Godwin and Britton's *Churches of London*. Note central three-decker pulpit, a rare feature

147   St Olave, Hart Street, in 1941, looking north-west

148   St Olave, Hart Street, as restored 1953. Note Mrs Pepys' monument by east window

door), the last two skilfully restored. Last but not least, the charming bust (removed for safety in war) on monument erected by Samuel Pepys to his wife Elizabeth in 1667[1] (above Bayning monument). Pepys, who was Clerk of the Acts (Secretary to the Navy Board) at the Navy Office then in Seething Lane and a frequent worshipper in this his parish church, had no monument until 1884, when one designed by Sir Arthur Blomfield was placed on south wall where the Navy Officers' Gallery was before 1854, which was reached by a staircase in the churchyard. In the baptistery is the entrance to a small crypt said to be twelfth-century, with the unusual feature of a well. It has a groined vault of two bays and is fitted up as a chapel. In the ante-room is a small museum with many interesting items and with fine heraldic brasses and shields from monuments above staircase on west wall. Other remains of lost monuments in chapel itself. The vestry of 1662 happily survives – note ancient door, cheerful plaster angel on ceiling and recently cleaned painting of three figures in chiaroscuro (said to be by de Witte) on the overmantle. Entrance to burial ground[2] in Seething Lane, dated 1658, with its skulls and spikes is an almost exact copy of a plate in a Dutch copy-book of 1633 and is mentioned by Charles Dickens in his *Uncommercial Traveller* under the name of 'St Ghastly Grim'.

P.W.   ST PETER, CORNHILL. Wren 1677–87.
This church is evidently of great antiquity, but not so old as is claimed for it on a celebrated brass tablet (said to date originally from time of Henry IV, 1399–1413), now in the vestry. This inscription states that St Peter was founded A.D. 179 as an Archbishop's Church by King Lucius, a mythical personage said to have reigned 77 years. This famed antiquity has gained St Peter several privileges, such as, in 1417 and long after, that of having the place of honour for its rector in the great Whitsuntide procession of City clergy to St Paul's and in 1860, when the Union of Benefices Act was passed (under which so many City churches have been demolished), St Peter was expressly excluded from it. As at St Michael, Cornhill, the houses on its north side (next the street), are built on site of former burial-ground apparently sold under Edward VI (1547–1553) and like St Michael there is

still a churchyard on the south side. In the fifteenth century a grammar school was established at St Peter – one of four ordered to be maintained in the City in 1425. There was also a library, repaired by Sir John Crosby,[3] which was afterwards occupied by the school up to the Great Fire. Wren's church is ten feet shorter than its predecessor, due to widening of Gracechurch Street. The east façade is a striking design with its five windows in a row and three above, while the tall brick tower has triple openings on each side of the belfry and fine dome and spire crowned with a key for vane, the emblem of the patron saint.[4] The attractive doorway from Cornhill leads into vestibule under organ gallery, with fine organ, originally by Father Smith. In this vestibule note between two fine doorcases, spacious bread-shelves, and, below, an ornate foreign chest seat; also, in the church, fine font and pulpit. The screen across the building is one of the only two in Wren's churches.[5] East end is rendered dark by ugly Victorian glass, while in the nave are four modern windows commemorating military units – those on the south the Bedfordshire and Hertfordshire Regiment (1951) and the Fifth Army (1959) and, on the north, the Royal Tank Regiment (1960). In vestry, note fine long table of seventeenth-century date, also old keyboard of the organ, on which Mendelssohn played, together with his autograph, dated 3 September 1840. On south wall is pathetic monument with seven cherubs' heads, commemorating a family of seven children burnt to death in 1782 while their father was at a ball at St James's Palace. George Borrow, author of *The Bible in Spain*, was married here in 1840.

P.   ST SEPULCHRE WITHOUT NEWGATE, Holborn Viaduct. Church of the Holy Sepulchre.
Partly pre-Fire, partly rebuilt 1667–70, it is said by Wren, but he appears to have had little, if anything, to do with it.[6] Largest parish church in City. First

---

[1] Unfortunately without its shaped black marble background.
[2] Now a quiet garden, rearranged 1970, when two limes were felled.
[3] See St Helen.
[4] As at St Lawrence Jewry.
[5] See St Margaret, Lothbury.
[6] Wren Soc. says it is by Wren, 1670–77.

mention 1137. Rebuilt in fifteenth century largely by Sir John Popham; the fine three-storey porch with fan-vault to ground floor is of this time, although refaced outside. Note fine iron gate. Fifteenth-century windows of church remained until 1790 when they were replaced by round-headed ones, only to be converted to Gothic again in 1878 – and the tower, which had lost most of its ancient beauty, was entirely refashioned and its pinnacles unduly enlarged. Interior has fine ranges of columns of Wren's time but the ceiling dates from *c*.1836. Galleries with carved fronts on north, south and west of church were demolished in the 1878 'restoration' when the splendid organ by Renatus Harris was moved from its proper west position and placed in north (St Stephen Harding) chapel, completely filling it up – it was enclosed by a dreadful stone screen, now mercifully removed. In 1930/32 the organ was moved again and rebuilt in the north aisle incorporating parts of the original, including the west front of the case (south front is Victorian), and the chapel restored to its proper use. Notice, beneath organ, carved panels from galleries, also two pulpits (the lower one, the reading desk, the higher the pulpit proper), the font and beautiful seventeenth-century reredos, fine iron altar-rails,[1] many charming memorials on pillars and walls and Royal Arms of 1714–1800 at west end of south aisle. Also, handbell (in glass case) with which watchmen of St Sepulchre's roused condemned prisoners of Newgate on eve of an execution; when they said: 'All you that in the condemned hole do lie, prepare you, for tomottow you shall die. Watch all and pray; the hour is drawing near That you before the Almighty must Appear. Examine well yourselves, in time, repent, That you may not to eternal flames be sent. And when St Sepulchre's Bell in the morning tolls, The Lord Have mercy on your souls. Past twelve o'clock'.[2] This custom, which died out in the early nineteenth century, originated in a bequest of £50 made by Robert Dow, 1605. John Rogers, vicar of this church, was burnt as a heretic, 1555. Robert Ascham, tutor to Queen Elizabeth, was buried here, 1568, and Captain John Smith, governor of Virginia was here interred, 1631. Note window to his memory in south aisle. Church escaped serious damage in last war, but vestry and famous Watch House, 1792, were

destroyed, the latter rebuilt 1962 and bust of Charles Lamb (formerly at Christ Church, Newgate Street) placed here. In 1946 was unveiled a stained glass window in memory of Sir Henry Wood, founder and conductor for fifty years of the Promenade Concerts. His father was a chorister, and here as a child he learnt to play the organ. Since 1964, four more windows have been added (to St Stephen Harding, Walter Carrel, Dame Nellie Melba, and John Ireland, the last two by Brian Thomas), so making this 'Musicians' Chapel a blaze of colour. The Cecilian Festival is now an annual event (22 November). Fine font cover from Christ Church, Newgate Street now in vestibule. St Sepulchre was repaired and decorated, a new east window inserted 1949, and the following year the south aisle dedicated as a memorial chapel for the Royal Fusiliers (City of London Regiment), for whom also the adjoining churchyard had been laid out as a Garden of Remembrance. The church was again decorated in 1967.

P.W. ST STEPHEN WALBROOK, next to Mansion House. Wren, 1672–77; steeple, 1717.
Dome wrecked May, 1941. Restored 1954. First mention *c*.1100. Originally on west bank of Walbrook (which runs under street of that name), but in 1429–39, with much laying of foundation stones, St Stephen was rebuilt on the east bank. This second church was larger than that so beautifully rebuilt by Wren. Present church is certainly one of his masterpieces and in its oblong interior he has contrived a cruciform arrangement with 16 pillars (eight of which uphold the dome) which also form a nave and four aisles. There is a recess at west end for the organ (first erected 1765) which has a rococo case. This harmonized well with the earlier fittings of Wren's time – the fine semi-elliptical altar-rails and table, magnificent pulpit and tester, and font with elaborate cover, which were bricked up and so saved from destruction during the war. Tower has steeple somewhat like those of St James Garlickhithe and St Michael Royal. A little house, formerly the clerk's house and later a bookseller's

---

[1] Others at St Botolph, Aldgate, St Mary Woolnoth and St Magnus.

[2] From an inscription beneath bell.

shop, was against it until the blitz. Slope of the ground to Walbrook shown by steps up to west entrance. Henry Chicheley, later Archbishop of Canterbury, was rector here, 1396–7 – his brother, Robert Chicheley, twice Lord Mayor, was largely responsible for the rebuilding of 1429. John Dunstable, musician, 1453, was buried here as was in 1668 Nathaniel Hodges, physician and hero of the plague year, 1665[1]; both have monuments. Sir John Vanbrugh, architect, playwright and Clarenceux, King of Arms, was also interred here. Upper part of dome destroyed in raids, but skilfully made good and whole interior restored by Godfrey Allen and re-dedicated 29 March 1954. In December 1961 three east windows were filled with stained glass of rich colour but obscure design by Keith New. They are said to represent, left, the Stoning of St Stephen, right, the Conversion of St Paul and, centre, the Crucified and Risen Christ. St Stephen is London H.Q. of 'The Telephone Samaritans' who work to prevent suicide, a world-wide organization founded by the present rector, Rev. Chad Varah. In churchyard at east end of St Stephen note 25 ledger stones, formerly on floor of church.

ST VEDAST, FOSTER LANE, Cheapside. Wren, 1695–1700; steeple 1709–12.
Burnt out December 1940. Restored 1962. Earliest mention *c.*1170. Dedication very rare – now only one other in England, at Tathwell, Lincs.[2] St Vedast was bishop of Arras in France (d. 540). Curiously enough, Foster Lane is a corruption of Vedast Lane by such steps as Vastes, Fastes, Faster, Faister and Fauster, as has been demonstrated by comparison of successive references. Robert Herrick the poet, son of a goldsmith of Cheapside, was baptized in the old church, 1591. Wren's church had a fine plaster ceiling and some beautiful fittings, especially the pulpit and altar-piece. This last had six cherubs carved in the round, holding torches or palms, and its loss is a heavy one. The elegant steeple is one of Wren's happiest works, unusual in having no urns, but relying for effect on its contrasting surfaces and cornices – concave and convex – with strongly emphasized angles. It is recorded that this steeple was pre-fabricated at Greenwich and brought by river at a cost of £50, as it could not be constructed in the small church-

yard (St Paul's Cathedral Library, MS, W.E. 15). Attached to the north side of the church was a contemporary cloister or colonnade with tiny rooms over, which escaped destruction. It led to a building of same date, formerly the parochial school and later the temporary church. It is curious that these buildings, although belonging to St Vedast, are in another parish and ward. Long under restoration by Dykes Bower, St Vedast was at length re-dedicated on 25 April 1962, and is fitted up with facing seats like a college chapel. Besides the font from St Anne & St Agnes, it was fortunate in obtaining three other pieces of Wren period furniture – organ case from St Bartholomew-by-the-Exchange (dem. 1841), reredos apparently from St Christopher-le-Stocks (dem. 1781) and pulpit from All Hallows, Bread Street (dem. 1878), which has two modern strips of symbolical carving. Note Stuart Royal Arms, north of altar (shield repainted with current Arms). The south aisle, which together with the east end, has been internally made rectangular within diverging exterior walls, is fitted up as a chapel (note fine old Holy Table), and both here and on the north wall of the church a number of monuments have been tastefully reinstated. The ceiling is perhaps unique in having not only gilding but also aluminium paint to enhance its beauties! Three east windows were designed by Brian Thomas – the lunette, with a Glory and Cherubs, at the west end of the aisle was originally in the top of the centre east window. The school and cloister, etc., have been very largely renewed and a fine rectory built on the west side of the little churchyard, now laid out as an attractive garden.

CHURCH EXISTING BUT NO LONGER IN CITY

ST MARY ALDERMANBURY. Wren, 1672–87, Victorianized.
Burnt out December, 1940, now rebuilt in the U.S.A. The suffix (name of street) means the 'bury' or court of the alderman. First mention of church 1181. Shakespeare's fellow-actors, Condell and

[1] See Bell's *Great Plague of London*, 1924.
[2] There was formerly another in Norwich.

149   St Vedast as restored 1962

150   St Mary Aldermanbury. Now rebuilt in U.S.A.

Hemmings, editors of the First Folio, 1623, were buried in the old church and are commemorated by a memorial in the churchyard, and Milton here married his second wife, Katherine Woodcocke, in 1656. Edmund Calamy, the Presbyterian, was minister of St Mary from 1639 until the Restoration; his son, Benjamin Calamy, was incumbent, 1677–83, and his grandson, Dr Edmund Calamy, a Non-conformist, was buried here in 1732. The notorious Judge Jeffreys and some of his family were also buried here, it is said, in a vault under the high altar. But when this was inspected after the war by Professor W.F. Grimes, no trace of the judge was found, the vault being appropriated to a Dyer family.[1] After the bombing St Mary was thought to have no future but in 1965/66 was taken down, the stones numbered and shipped to America.

There in the campus of Westminster College, Fulton, Missouri, they have been assembled and the church rebuilt as nearly as possible to the original design, but raised on a basement under the direction of Marshall Sisson and Professor Patrick Horsburgh. It was at this college that Sir Winston Churchill delivered his famous Sinews of Peace (or Iron Curtain) speech in 1946 and the rebuilt St Mary forms a memorial to him and the war-time cooperation between Britain and the U.S.A. which he did so much to foster. It was consecrated by the bishop of London on 7 May 1969. Since the removal, the foundations of the tower, outer walls and columns, as used by Wren,

---

[1] Vaults under the nave, it seems, have not been investigated.

still *in situ* have been excavated, and the site attractively laid out.

OTHER CHURCHES

TEMPLE CHURCH, Fleet Street (St Mary). 12th and 13th centuries, much restored.

Burnt out May, 1941. Restored 1954–58. This was the church of the London house of the Order of Knights Templar, founded in 1118 to protect pilgrims to the holy places in Jerusalem. They came to Fleet Street from Holborn, at the time of Henry II (1154–89), and the church was consecrated in 1185 by Heraclius, Patriarch of Jerusalem, who also the same year hallowed that of the Hospitallers of St John, in Clerkenwell. Like other churches of these military monks, the Temple Church was made circular in imitation of that of the Holy Sepulchre in Jerusalem,[1] the present choir being added in 1240 in 'Early English' or first pointed style, the 'Round' being transitional from Norman with round-headed windows and pointed arches. The elaborate doorway, much restored, is the only ornamented Norman entrance in Inner London. Wren furnished St Mary's with pews and a beautiful organ screen (between Round and choir), pulpit and reredos but all these were swept away in 1840 when the church was drastically renovated, and all the monuments of post-Reformation date deposited in the triforium of the Round (upper storey of aisle)! The famous effigies, many of them cross-legged (which does not indicate a journey to Palestine), had been much 'restored' and were terribly injured when the church was burnt. Whom they represent is not certainly known, but they exhibit fine examples of military accoutrements of the twelfth and thirteenth centuries.[2] For long covered up, they have now been exposed and as far as possible carefully restored, but three or four were found to be so calcined as to be featureless. But of the other monuments, the Plowden memorial, 1585, and that of Richard Martin, 1615, brought down from triforium between the wars, were bricked up and are intact. After suppression of the Templars in 1312, the Temple was eventually granted to the Hospitallers who leased it to the students of Law, at the time of Edward III (1327–77) who have retained it ever since, they having acquired the freehold in the seventeenth century. St Mary is now joint chapel of the Societies of the Inner and Middle Temple, two of the four Inns of Court which have exclusive right of admitting persons to practice at the bar, who thereby become barristers. The choir was re-opened 23 March 1954 with the organ presented by Lord Glentanar in enlarged chamber on north side and the Wren altar-piece reinstated after long residence in Bowes Museum, Barnard Castle, Co. Durham. The nave followed on 7 November 1958. The Master's House north-east of the church, destroyed in air raids, has been rebuilt.

AUSTIN FRIARS, near Old Broad Street. Pre-Fire.

Destroyed by direct hit, October 1940; now rebuilt. This was the nave of the church of a monastery of Augustine Friars, founded in 1253. It was rebuilt a century later and Stow says it had 'A most fine spired steeple, small, high, and straight, I have not seen the like'. At the dissolution of the monasteries under Henry VIII the choir and crossing were granted to Wm. Paulet, 1st marquess of Winchester, and survived until *c*.1611. But the nave was given by Edward VI to Dutch and Flemish Protestants, the former of whom continued to use it until its destruction in the war. By them it was known as 'Jesus Temple'. In 1862 a fire consumed the roof and all the old fittings, and after the consequent 'restoration', little survived of original work other than the tall and graceful fourteenth-century arcades and the floor, mostly composed of memorial slabs unfortunately all destroyed at the rebuilding. The new church, by Arthur Bailey (opened 1954), is less than half the size of the old structure. Of the rest of the site, part was sold and part utilized for secular buildings in connection with the church. The stained glass is varied and striking, especially the great west window by Max Nanta. Those at the east end are by Hugh Easton, and the nice little heraldic panels in the north aisle

---

[1] Other examples remaining being at Cambridge, Northampton and Little Maplestead, Essex.

[2] Among those known to have been buried here, and who may be represented by some of the effigies, were Geof de Magnaville, earl of Essex, 1144, and the great Wm. Mareschal, earl of Pembroke (d. 1219) and two of his sons. Also one of the effigies must be that of a De Ros, from the arms on his shield (three 'water bougets' or skin bottles).

by W. M. Wilson. The sculpture is by John Skeaping and Esmond Burton.

TOWERS REMAINING

ALL HALLOWS STAINING, Mark Lane. Pre-Fire, Victorianized.
Formed part of old church that fell down, 1671, and was rebuilt, apparently not by Wren. Church demolished 1870, except tower, which was drastically 'restored'. (See St Olave, Hart Street.)

ST ALBAN, WOOD STREET. Wren's Gothic, 1682–87 and 1697–8.
Burnt out December, 1940. Probably of Saxon foundation and is stated to have been a chapel of King Offa (d. 796). Rebuilt 1633–4, it is said by Inigo Jones; some of this church surviving the Great Fire was incorporated by Wren in his re-building. Apse added by Scott, 1858, in place of old east window. Parapet and pinnacles of tower coarsely renewed *c*.1878. On pulpit was a beautiful seventeenth-century hourglass on brass stand, fortunately rescued and now at St Vedast. The church has been demolished, except for the tower which is now in the middle of the street.

ST ALPHEGE, LONDON WALL, near Cripplegate. Pre-Fire.
The original St Alphege was on north side of street against City wall (churchyard remains), but at the Reformation, due to its being ruinous, the parishioners abandoned it and obtained possession of church of newly dissolved Elsing Priory, dating from the fourteenth century, of which the crossing and lower part of central tower remains. The chancel, which formed the parish church, was rebuilt 1777 only to be demolished 1924, leaving the tower, with its pretentious porch (built 1914) as a chapel which became derelict. Contained numerous monuments, that to Sir Rowland Hayward, Lord Mayor 1570 and 1591, being particularly fine, but later wrecked by hooligans. The porch is now demolished and the mediaeval work preserved as a ruin.

ST AUGUSTINE, WATLING STREET. Wren, 1680–87; steeple, 1695–98.
First mentioned 1145. Burnt out 1941 and for a time temporary church was under tower, which is oblong in plan and has elaborate pinnacled and pierced parapet. It carried an attractive lead-covered spire, destroyed in the blitz, as were also the fine reredos (Victorianized) and charming font. Church now demolished and new Choir School for St Paul's (opened 1967) built over the site, but the tower is retained and a new spire, reproducing the original design (altered 1829), was added in 1966 – the upper part in fibre-glass.

ST MARTIN ORGAR, Martin Lane, Cannon Street. Modern.
Burnt in 1666, the parish was united to St Clement Eastcheap, but the church not being wholly destroyed, was patched up and used by a French Protestant congregation until 1820, when it was demolished except for the tower. This survived until 1851, when it too was pulled down. Strange to relate, a new tower, far loftier than the old, was erected on the site and still stands, but bereft of its original pyramidal roof. It carries a projecting clock. The old churchyard remains.

ST MARY SOMERSET, Upper Thames Street. Wren.
Church demolished *c*.1871, except for tower which was remarkable for crown of tall obelisks and urns, parts of which were taken down after the war for safety as apparently they were weakened by blast. These have now been replaced and the whole tower very carefully restored by the City Corporation, who are responsible for its upkeep. Before the war, the tower was used as a rest room for women during the lunch hour. The south churchyard was destroyed with the church, but the one to the north survived until the blitz.

ST OLAVE JEWRY. Wren.
Church demolished 1887 or 1888, except tower which after some alterations was converted into entrance to offices and a dwelling house (sometime rectory of St Margaret, Lothbury, to which church

the parish is united).[1] On destruction of these buildings in the war, portions of mediaeval walling of the eastern part of the church were exposed and could be seen from Old Jewry. Churchyard remains.

TOWER EXISTING BUT NO LONGER IN CITY

ALL HALLOWS, LOMBARD STREET. Wren.
Was one of the few City churches known to date from before Norman Conquest, being given in 1053 to Christchurch, Canterbury. It stood behind the houses at corner of Lombard Street and Gracechurch Street, being approached by covered passages from both and so was nicknamed the 'Church Invisible'. Was demolished 1939 and the tower re-erected the next year at Twickenham as a campanile to a new church, by Messrs Anderson & Atkinson, F.F.R.I.B.A. to which it is joined by a covered way. Most of the monuments and very fine fittings have been transferred there and should be visited. John Wesley preached his first extempore sermon in All Hallows in 1735.

---

[1] The vane, a ship in full sail, came from St Mildred, Poultry (dem. 1871). It was bent by blast but has now been straightened.

Bibliography

ABBREVIATIONS

Accs.	Accounts
Ant. Journ.	Antiquaries' Journal
Arch.	Archaeologia
A.A.Akt.Bk.	Architectural Association's Sketch Books (1870s–*c*.1920)
A.R.	Architectural Review
B.A.A.	British Archaeological Association
B.	The Builder
Burl. Mag.	Burlington Magazine
Con.	Connoisseur
C.L.	Country Life
Dem.	Demolished
Des.	Destroyed
Dps	Double page spread
Gents. Mag.	Gentleman's Magazine (1731–1860s)
G.F.	Great Fire of 1666
I.L.N.	Illustrated London News
L.C.C.	London County Council
L & M Ar. Soc.	London & Middlesex Archaeological Society
L. Top. R.	London Topographical Record
P.p.	privately printed
St P's Ecc. Soc.	St Paul's Ecclesiological Society
temp.	at the time of
Top.	topography or topographical
V. Mins.	Vestry Minutes

1. GENERAL

THE CITY CHURCHES BEFORE THE GREAT FIRE I

Victoria County History: London, Vol 1, 1909, pp. 171–406. Ecclesiastical history – parish churches and dissenting chapels. 4 folding plans of City to show churches at different periods

H.A. Harben A Dictionary of London, 1918. Valuable for earliest references, derivations of names, etc. Lge 8to. Lge scale plan of City

H.B. Walters London Churches at the Reformation, 1939. Inventories temp. Edward VI. From documents in Public Record Office

John Stow Survey of London, 1598 and 1603. Edited by C.L. Kingsford. 2 vols, 1908, with plan of City. Supplement (booklet) 1927. 1633 edn – valuable information on churches of that time

Wilberforce Jenkinson London Churches before the Great Fire, 1917, with 20 collotypes, 12 of the City

J.G. White Churches and Chapels of Old London, 1901

Rev. Gordon Huelin The Pre-Fire City Churches, 1968. P.p. – to be had at St Margaret Pattens
The two last books deal with churches not rebuilt after the Great Fire.

CHURCHES BEFORE THE GREAT FIRE II: PAROCHIAL RECORDS ETC
Edwin Freshfield Between 1876 and 1895 Freshfield

produced 9 publications of parochial records:

St Stephen, Coleman Street from Arch. LV, 1887

St Margaret, Lothbury, St Christopher-le-Stocks and St Bartholomew-by-the-Exchange from Arch. XLV, 1876

4 of St Christopher-le-Stocks

2 of St Bartholomew-by-the-Exchange

1 of St Margaret, Lothbury

The last 7 were privately printed; all contain valuable information and some have interesting illustrations.

Henry Littlehales Mediaeval Records of a London City Parish – St Mary-at-Hill – 1420–1559. Early English Text Soc., 1905. 5 illus. 1 plan 3 facsimiles of pages and folded panorama of London in 1550

Rev. W. Sparrow Simpson Churchwardens' Accounts of St Matthew, Friday Street. B.A.A. Journal, 1869, pp. 356–381

A.J. Waterlow Accounts of the Churchwardens of St Michael, Cornhill, 1456–1608. P.p., *c*.1870. Illus.

Chas Welch Churchwardens Accs., All Hallows, London Wall, 1455–1536. P.p., 1912, with facsimile of Wynkyn de Worde's *The Fruit of Redemcyon* by Simon-the-Anker of London Wall, 1514

Rev. Gordon Huelin Article on Churchwardens' Accs., St Margaret Moses. Guildhall Studies in London History, Vol I, 1973

Walter G. Bell The Great Plague in London, 1665. 18 full-page plts, 5 folding plts, 1924

The Great Fire of London, 1666, 25 full-page plts, 3 folding, 1920. 3rd edn 1923. Both vivid descriptions of these disasters, *inter alia* for the churches.

THE CHURCHES GENERALLY

J. Peller Malcolm Londinium Redivivum: An Ancient History and Modern Description, derived from parochial records and personal inspection. Valuable, 4 vols, 4to, 1802–07

Thomas Allen History and Antiquities of London: Westminster & Southwark 4 vols, 8vo, 1828. Reprinted with extra vol 1838. Vol III, for City, valuable descriptions of churches by Edw. John Carlos

Laurence Gomme Gents. Mag. Library – topography. London, Vol I, 1904, pp. 206–26, 229–34 and Vol II, 1905, pp. 1–95. Notices of churches up to 1863, some of great value

George Godwin & John Britton The Churches of London (City only) 2 vols, 1838–39. Remarkable for patronizing attitude to Wren and his successors. Good illus.

John Timbs Curiosities of London, 1855. Latest edn 1885. Section on the churches pp. 101–216

A.H. Mackmurdo Wren's City Churches, 8vo or 4to, 1883. Remarkable: unique and often extravagant appreciation of Wren and his work

W. Niven London City Churches Demolished since 1800 or Now Threatened, 1887. Good plan of City and fine etchings

Last two books have interesting matter on demolition of the churches.

G.H. Birch London Churches of the 17th & 18th Centuries. Lge folio, 1896. Valuable illus. and plans

A.E. Daniell London City Churches, 1895. 2nd edn 1907 with good plan of City

T. Francis Bumpus London Churches, Ancient and Modern, 2 vols, 1908. 1st vol revised and issued as Ancient London Churches, 1910, and again *c*.1923

Philip Norman London City Churches that Escaped the Great Fire. Lon. Top. Rec., Vol v, 1908

Apart from literature inspired by the threat of demolition of 19 churches in 1920–26, a number of mostly slight publications were issued between 1913 and 1932, of varying degrees of inaccuracy. Of these 4 may be mentioned:

Margaret Tabor The City Churches; A Short Guide, 1917. Well arranged, illus. 2 good plans of City

G.B. Besant City Churches and Their Memories, 1927? Churches west of New Bridge St and Farringdon St omitted

M.V. Hughes The City Saints: A New Tour of Old London, 1932.

F. St Aubyn-Brisbane If Stones Could Speak, 1929. Lge 8vo, 352 pp. Anecdotal, generally unreliable and 'snapshot' illus.

L.C.C. Proposed Demolition of 19 City Churches, 1920, 24 plts, fine folding plan

The London Society The London City Churches, 1923; 2nd edn revd 1929. Notes on each church, tabular lists of services etc by the rectors, good folding plan

Mark Rogers Down Thames Street, 1921, 4to, many intersting drawings. Covers St Benet, Paul's Wharf, St James Garlickhithe, St Michael Royal, St Magnus, St Mary-at-Hill, St Dunstan-in-the-East

William Kent Encyclopaedia of London, 1937. Pp 99–206 The City Churches. Quick, interesting information

Elizabeth & Wayland Young Old London Churches, lge 8vo, 1951. Unreliable but with fine illus. The City, pp. 45–140 (includes many chapels)

Gerald Cobb Article, Our Heritage in the City Churches, in Occasional Paper No. 1 of Friends of the City Churches, 1944. Enlarged, with illus., Ecc. Soc. 1966

Rev. Basil Clarke Parish Churches of London, 1966, 4to. Pp 12–49, The City. 197 illus., 31 of City

R.G. Ellen (Master, Parish Clerks' Company, 1971–72) A London Steeple Chase: A Survey of the 150 Churches 'in the Bills of Mortality', 1972, 24 plts

M. and E. Quantrill Monuments of Another Age, Quartet Books, folio, 1975. Not reliable, illus. mostly poor but plans of Wren churches valuable

BOOKS AND ARTICLES WITH VALUABLE
ILLUSTRATIONS: GENERAL

West & Toms Churches That Escaped the Great Fire, 2 long albums, each of 12 engravings, 1736 and 1739. Valuable

Charles Clarke Architectura Ecclesiastica Londini, 1820, 4to or folio. 123 engravings, 78 of City churches from drawings by Coney, Shepherd, etc, of varying merit

Godwin & Britton Churches of London, 2 vols, 1838 and 39. Good illus., engraved or woodcut, of all City churches then standing

S.H.R. Salmon Artist in Photography, Series of valuable photographs of City church interiors, *c.*1885

G.H. Birch London Churches of the 17th & 18th Centuries, 1896. Lge folio, 64 collotypes of superb photos by Chas Latham, 41 of the City. Also 63 plans, 53 of City, and many other illus.

Canon Benham Old London Churches, 1908. 4to, 25 col. plts. From fine oil paintings by Arthur

Garrett, 18 of City

Pitkins Picture Books City of London Churches, All Hallows-by-the-Tower, St Mary-le-Bow, St Clement Danes, 1960s and 70s

See also *Niven*, City Churches Demolished Since 1800 p. 179 and *E. & W. Young*, Old London Churches, 1951, p. 180

COMPREHENSIVE PUBLICATIONS: GENERAL AND/OR
ARCHITECTURAL TEXT AND ILLUSTRATIONS

Royal Commission on Historical Monuments Inventory of the City, 1929. 4to, 348 photographic illus., 45 plans of churches

Gerald Cobb The Old Churches of London, 3 edns 1942–48, 8vo. Dedications of churches, etc, author's grouping of all Wren's steeples and many fine photographic and other illus.

Sir N. Pevsner The Buildings of England: London, Vol 1: The Cities of London and Westminster, 1957. 3rd edn, 1973, pp. 129–63 The City Churches

E.A. Webb St Bartholomew's Priory and Church, 1921, 2 vols, 102 plts, lge 8vo

London Survey Volumes

Vol IX 1924 St Helen Bishopgate Pt I 124 plts of church and fittings

Vol XII 1929 All Hallows, Barking Pt I 90 plts of churches

Vol XV 1934 All Hallows, Barking Pt II 120 plts, 49 of monuments in church

Monograph XV 1944 Church of St Bride, Fleet Street, 65 plts

WREN CHURCHES AND FITTINGS

THE BUILDING AND FURNISHING OF WREN'S
CHURCHES I

The Accounts

St Paul's Library Vols 36–39 in series W.D. Apparently the working copies of the accounts from 1670–1695, while in series W.E. 1–53 are similar accounts from the years 1695–1717 (with contracts and other relevant information) which establish the dates for most of the steeples. Virtually unknown until investigated by R.H. Harrison, F.S.A.

Bodleian, Oxford: Rawlinson MSS
  B387 The Bills of the Parochial Churches – the accounts
  B388 Ledger of the Parochial Churches – of little interest
  B389 Tabernacle Ledger and General Account – deals with the temporary accommodation before the rebuilding of churches
B387 is the fair copy of the first series of St Paul's Library accounts (1670–95) and these are dealt with in Arch. LXVI, 1914–15, in article by Lawrence Weaver, pp. 1–60, in which he gives full accounts for rebuilding St Mary-le-Bow and St Stephen Walbrook (except steeple). Reprinted in Wren Soc. Vol x.

For the fittings of the rebuilt churches see the Vestry Minutes and Churchwardens' Accounts of the various parishes, most of which are in the Guildhall Library where they may be inspected (see Hand Lists, published by the Library Committee). Extracts are printed in Vols x and xix of Wren Soc. Unfortunately, only those of the churches actually rebuilt were covered; those of the parishes united to them in 1670, containing interesting information, were overlooked.

Edw. Hatton New View of London, 1708. Detailed descriptions of new furniture in Wren's churches and of those that escaped the Fire. Valuable. Reprinted in Wren's Parentalia, 1750 and again in Wren Soc. Vol x

WREN'S CHURCHES II
R.H. Harrison Temporary Churches after the Great Fire. Article, Ecc. Soc., 1955–56
The Wren Society Vols IX, x and xix
Vol IX: frontispieces, plan of City and spread of Cockerell's Tribute to Sir Christopher Wren, 1838 (a grouping of his chief works). 20 old prints of demolished churches, 10 pp. of reproductions of Clayton's measured drawings of the churches, 43 plts of Wren drawings (37 of the City)
  Vol x: 60 pp. photographic views of churches, 23 plts of Wren drawings (15 of City), print of interior of St Stephen Walbrook
  Vol xix: 82 plts of which 12 are of old photographs and 3 of modern ones of the churches.

Grouping of all Wren's steeples by Gerald Cobb
Sir John Summerson Two articles on Wren drawings in the Bute Collection, R.I.B.A. Journal, 1952 and Journal of Soc. Architectural Historians, 1970. Also chapter on City churches in Pelican History of Art – Architecture in Britain, 1530–1830, 3rd edn, 1958
Viktor Furst The Architecture of Sir Christopher Wren, 1956. 4to, 197 illus., 64 of City churches
Eduard Seckler Wren and His Place in European Architecture, 1956. Lge 8vo, 80 plts, 35 of City churches, 74 figs, 47 plans of churches, 4 east ends and Cobb's grouping of all Wren steeples
The last two books are valuable for, *inter alia*, foreign sources of inspiration.
Margaret Whinney Wren, in World of Art Library, Thames & Hudson, 1971, pp. 45–80

Special Features
A.T. Taylor Towers and Steeples of Sir Christopher Wren, 1881, 13 plts of drawings
G.E. Francis 6 articles with fine illus. in A.R., *c.*1915, on Renaissance Steeples of London. Many of City
Laurence Weaver 3 articles in Burl. Mag., 1906–07. London's Leaded Steeples, 27 illus., 19 of City
Arthur Keen 2 articles in A.R., 1911, on ceilings of City churches, 11 photos, 18 plans or sections

WREN'S CHURCHES III: MEASURED DRAWINGS
Besides the Wren drawings in All Souls', Oxford, King's Library, British Museum etc (Wren Soc. Vols IX, x), there is in St Paul's Library a large folio album from the Crace Collection of many original 18th-century measured drawings of Wren's churches with a few later items.
John Clayton Parochial Churches of Sir Christopher Wren. Elephant folio, 1848. 60 double-page lithos of measured drawings of 46 churches. Rearranged and reproduced on 70 pp. of Wren Soc. Vol IX
Arthur Stratton 4 articles in Architecture, 1897, on Wren's City churches. Fine measured drawings by author
A.E. Richardson Article in A.R., 1910: A Minor City Church – St Benet, Paul's Wharf. 7 illus. incl. elevations, sections and plan (these last

reprinted in Builder, 1916 and Architects' Journal, 1923)

In the Architectural Association's Sketch Books (issued annually between 1870s and *c.*1920) are measured drawings of Wren and other City churches and church fittings, as also in Builder and other architectural periodicals.

Walter H. Godfrey Monograph XV of London Survey volumes, 1944: Church of St Bride, Fleet Street. 4to, 65 plts.

CITY CHURCH FITTINGS

Edw. Hatton New View of London, 1708. See 'Sources' above

Christopher Hussey Article 27.11.1926 in Country Life on craftsmanship of City churches, 12 illus. See also his article on menaced City churches, C.L. 13.11.1926

Edwin Freshfield Communion Plate in the Churches of the City of London, 1894. 4to, 15 collotypes (8 of beadles' staves), 32 half-tone groups of plate

Illustrated London News Double page spread of plate from City churches from V & A Exhibition. Issue of 7.12.1946

Mary and Charlotte Thorpe London Church Staves, 1895. Many poor drawings, incl. 15 of City staves

Edwin Freshfield Article in Arch. LIV, p. 41, on sword stands in churches in City, 6 fine collotypes

Mrs L.B. Ellis Article in Lon. & Middx. Arch. Soc. Vol X. Royal Hatchments in City Churches

R.H. Harrison Article in Ancient Mons. Sco. N.S. Vol 8, 1960. Dispersed Fittings of the City Churches

C.W. Pearce Notes on Old City Churches, Their Organs, Organists and Musical Associations, 1909

Stained Glass

Three slight publications:

Ancient Stained and Painted Glass in London in *Pages from the Past* series of paperbacks, 1939

Sydney Eden, The Lost Stained Glass Treasures of London, reprinted from Wm Kent's Lost Treasures of London, 1947[1]

John A. Knowles Article in Antiquaries Journal, 1953, The Price Family of Glass Painters

Parochial Records are generally valuable for information:

1. Churchwardens' Accounts and Vestry Minutes. See 'Churches before the Great Fire' and 'Building of Wren's Churches-Sources'. These books were often beautifully written and many of the accounts were elaborately decorated, as were those of St Botolph, Aldgate, St James Garlickhithe, St Margaret Pattens, St Mildred, Bread Street, etc.

2. Registers of Baptisms, Marriages and Burials. From 1538 it was enacted that all parish churches should keep such records, and most of those of the City churches have been printed. They are of course of great value to genealogists. See Lon. & Middx. Arch. Soc. N.S. Vol 8 for list of printed registers – Parish Registers for London and Middlesex by C.W.F. Goss.

3. BOOKS AND ARTICLES ON INDIVIDUAL CHURCHES

Gent's Mag. 1831, p. 217. Letter from E.I.C. (Ed. John Carlos) re. repairs to 5 churches: St A. Undershaft, St Augustine, St Antholin, St B. Aldersgate, Austin Friars. See also p. 189

Holy Trinity Minories
Rev. Samuel Kinns Six Hundred Years, or Historical Sketches of H.T.M., 1898. Many illus., 12 of church monuments, personnel
E.M. Tomlinson A History of the Minories, 1907 and 1922. 13 plts

Holy Trinity, Gough Square (dem. 1913)
Godwin & Britton Vol II of Churches of London
L. Russell Muirhead Article in Middx Quarterly and London County Review, Winter, 1954, p. 8 – A Short-lived City Church

Christ Church, Newgate Street
P. Norman Article, St Paul's Eccl. Soc. Vol VII, p. 32

All Hallows, Barking
Rev. Joseph Maskell Parochial History and Antiquities of A.H.B., 1864. Sml 4to
Rev. Canon Mason Article, Berkyngechirche in the 19th Century, 1894. Reprinted 1927, 1938

---

[1] In Journal of Brit. Soc. of Master Glass Painters, Vol X, 1947.

Rev. C.R.D. Biggs Berkyngechurch by the Tower, 1899. The story and work of A.H.B. 8vo

Montague H. Cox & P. Norman Part 1 London Survey Vol XII, 1929, 90 plts; Part 2 London Survey Vol XV, 1934, 49 plts of monuments

A Vade Mecum For the Friends of A.H. by the Tower: Booklet, rev. edn 1936

Charles Spon Berkyngechirche: A.H.B. Past and Present, 1941. Booklet, 2nd edn 1944, 19 good illus. 2 plans

G.C. Misselbrook Monumental Brasses of A.H.B. 1953, 17 illus.

All Hallows, Lombard Street & All Hallows, Twickenham

Halsey Ricardo Article, Arch. Review Vol XIII on threatened demolition of A.H.L.S. 12 fine illus, E. Dockree, photographer

P. Norman Article, St Paul's Eccl. Soc. Vol v, p. 265

Miss Jeffries Davis A City Church in Danger, Journal London Soc., Jan 1936

City Churches Preservation Society Shall All Hallows Be Destroyed? Booklet, 1936. Valuable info. re scheme to unite A.H. & St Edmund, Lombard Street

Rev. J.H.A. Charles Booklet by vicar of A.H.T., 1959. Plan of parish, 9 illus.

All Hallows, London Wall

Churchwardens' Accounts 1455–1536 – See p. 179

Rev. Montague-Fowler History of A.H.L.W., c.1908, 96 pp.

Guild Church of A.H. on the Wall: A Christian Art Centre for the City of London, c.1962. Now discontinued as such

All Hallows Staining

Rev. A. Povah Annals of St Olave, Hart St.: chs XIX–XXII (pp. 315–372) on A.H.S.

St Alphege

Church and Tower of St A. Article in Arch. Review, 1907. Measured drawings by E. Gunn

Pierson C. Carter History of Church and Parish of St A. London Wall, 1925 4to P.p.

St Andrew-by-the-Wardrobe

R.H. Harrison Article in Ecc. Soc., 1954, p. 163. Rebuilding of St A.W. after Great Fire of 1666

R.H. Harrison Booklet on St Anne's Vestry Hall, 1949 – then used as temporary church for St A.W.

Ivor Bulmer-Thomas Booklet St A.W., 1966 2nd edn 1969

St Andrew Undershaft

G.H. Birch Article in St Paul's Eccl. Soc. Vol I 1881–5 (read 1882)

P. Norman Article in St Paul's Eccl. Soc. Vol v 1900–05. Reprinted Lon. Top. Record, Vol v, 1908, p. 67

C.B. Boulter History of St A., 1935 Many interesting illus.

St Anne & St Agnes

Wm. McMurray A City Church Chronicle: A Short History of St. A & St A. and St John Zachary, 1914. Booklet, 80 pp.

Wm. McMurray Records of Two City Parishes (St A. & St A. and St J.Z.), 1925. Valuable book but horribly produced and bound. 500 pp.

R. Percival Notes and Extracts relating to St A. & St A. Church, 1966. 4to pamphlet 2 illus.

St Antholin

A. Chas. Knight Cordwainer Ward in the City of London, 1917. Article IV, Churches of the Ward: St A. pp. 38–42 (For St A.'s Lectures see p. 162, note 1)

St Augustine

See first item this section

St Bartholomew-by-the-Exchange

Articles in Gents. Mag., 1840, Pt 1, p. 462. Also 1841 Pt 1, p. 153 – E.I.C.

Freshfield's Vestry Minutes, 1890 and Account Books, 1895, see p. 179

St Bartholomew-the-Great

Article in *Wilkinson's* Londina Illustrata, 1821–22. Lge 4to. Fine folded plan and other plts

J.H. Parker Articles in Gents. Mag., 1863, Pt 2, pp. 391–406 and 623–29.

Geo. Worley Priory Church of St B.G., 1908. Bell's Greater Church series

E. Aston Webb Records of St B., Smithfield, 1921, 2 vols, lge 8vo. Outstanding work. 102 plts inc. plans and measured drawings

St Bartholomew-the-Less

Article in *Wilkinson's* Londina Illustrata, 1834. Fine plates

L.J. Douglas Article in St B. Hospital Journal, Oct. 1936, with 'plan' of church in 1617

Gweneth Whitteridge Royal Hospital of St B. Booklet, c.1952

St Benet Fink
 H.G. Article in Gents. Mag., 1836, pp. 256–59
 E.I.C. (Ed. John Carlos) Article in Gents. Mag., 1840, pp. 463–64
St Benet, Paul's Wharf (Welsh Church)
 Basil Champneys Article in Portfolio, 1871, p. 106 Under 'Churches About Queen Victoria Street'
 H.R. Plomer Article on Vestry Minutes in Home Counties Mag., 1909, p. 120
 P. Norman Article in St Paul's Eccl. Soc. Vol VII, p. 27, 1911
 Francis Steer Guild Church of St B.P.W. Booklet, 1970. V. good account, chiefly of monuments, with dps of 4 measured drawings and 4 plans of church
St Botolph, Aldersgate
 Rev. J. Selby Henery St B. without Aldersgate, its Church and Parish Records, 1895, 17 plts
St Botolph, Aldgate
 Rev. A.G.B. Atkinson St B.A.: the Story of a City Parish, 1898. 244 pp, last chapter by Rev. R.H. Haddon, vicar
St Botolph, Bishopsgate
 Article in Church Monthly, 1907. p. 204. 3 illus.
St Bride, Fleet Street
 Article in Gents. Mag., 1825, Pt I, pp. 17–20
 Rev. E.C. Hawkins Church and Parish of St B.F.S., 1905
 W.H. Godfrey London Survey Committee monograph 15, 1944. 65 plts
 G. Cobb The Church of St B.F.S. 4to booklet, 1951. 3 plts
 Rev. C.M. Armitage Beauty for Ashes, 1952. 4to booklet in aid of restoration fund. 8 plts
 W.M. Redpath Chronicles of St B. I: Fleet Street's Church Restored, 1940–57. Pamphlet 1958, 2nd edn 1959, 7 plts
 Rev. Dewi Morgan St B.F.S. in City of London. Tall booklet by vicar, 1969. Rev. 1973. Many fine illus.
 Rev. Dewi Morgan Phoenix of Fleet Street: 200 Years of St B., 1973, 290 pp. 278 illus. (18 in colour)
St Clement Eastcheap
 Rev. W.E. Lees St C.'s Church near E., 1937, 9 illus.
St Dionis Backchurch
 G.E. Street Remains of Mediaeval Crypt at

St D. Article in Builder, 1858, p. 508
 A.R. Winnett History of St D.B. and St D., Parsons Green, 1935, 5 plts
St Dunstan-in-the-East
 New church – 3 articles in Gents. Mag., 1821 Pt I, pp. 35, 81 & 297
 Rev. T.B. Murray Chronicles of a City Church, by rector, 1859. Sml 4to 89 pp.
 Rev. A.G.B. West Church and Parish of St D. in E. Booklet by rector, c.1930, 100 pp.
 Rev. J. Wall 12-page pamphlet by priest-in-charge, 1953
St Dunstan-in-the-West
 Rev. J.F. Denham Views... of Exterior & Interior and Principal Monuments . . . of St D. in W. 1831. V. lge 4to, 33 pp., 5 lithographs
 The New Church. Article in Gents. Mag., 1832, pp. 297–302
 St D-in-the-W., Fleet Street – Booklet, 1968 and earlier
St Edmund
 R.H. Harrison St E. King & Martyr, 1960. Booklet by Ecc. Soc.
St Ethelburga
 P. Norman Article, Lon. Top. Record Vol V (1908) p. 93
 Rev. W.F. Cobb (later Geikie-Cobb) Some Notes on . . . St E. the Virgin. The Press of the Church of St E. Booklet, 1904
 B.R. Leftwich A Short History & Guide to ... St E., 1948. Booklet, photo of old interior, 1860s (misprinted 1890)
St Giles Cripplegate
Wm. Muller London before 1666. With account of parish, ward & church of St G.C. Sml 8vo, 1867, pp. 43–92
 Rev. W. Denton Records of St G.C., 1883. Deals with whole parish; church pp. 21–43
 J.J. Baddeley Church & Parish of St G. without C. Interesting illus., esp. monuments and facsimiles. Lge 8vo, 1888
St Helen, Bishopsgate
 Rev. J.E. Cox Annals of St H.B., 1876. Lge 8vo, 454 pp., 16 illus. inc. 2 plans
 Minnie Redan & A.W. Clapham Church of St H.B. London Survey Vol IX, 1924. 124 plts, 2 coloured
 G.H. Birch Article in St Paul's Eccl. Soc. Vol I,

c.1883

Anon Short Account of St H.B. Booklet, 1930. p. 21 mentions ms History of St H. 2 vols in oak cabinet – given to church by children of author – *Wm. Meade Williams*, 1922

Folio folder of brass rubbings from St H. 10 plts On sale in church

St James Garlickhithe

P. Norman St Paul's Eccl. Soc. Vol VI, 1906–10

Marjorie Honeybourne Short Account of St J.G., 1952, 1965

St Katherine Cree

P. Norman Article, St Paul's Eccl. Soc. Vol V, 1900–05, p. 189. Reprinted in Lon. Top. Record Vol V, 1908

St Lawrence Jewry (See also p. 187)

P. Norman Article, St Paul's Eccl. Soc. Vol V, p. 261

R.W. Wilson St L.J. next Guildhall. Booklet, *c*.1938?

Andrew Freeman & Noel Mander St L. next Guildhall: A History of the Organs, 4to booklet, 1957

St Lawrence Pountney

Rev. H.B. Wilson History of the Parish of St L.P., 1831. 4to, 228 pp.

St Magnus

P. Norman Article in St Paul's Eccl. Soc. Vol VII, p. 121

St Margaret Lothbury

Anon Sml booklet *c*.1966 based on *Rev. Wm. Priest*'s Some Historical Notes on St M.L., 1930

St Margaret Pattens

Guild Church of St M.P.: Short Account of Restoration, 1955–56. Pamphlet

History of Organ, St M.P. Booklet, 1958

Rev. Dr Huelin St M. in Eastcheap: A City Parish in the 19th Century. Guildhall Misc., 1971

St Martin, Ludgate

P. Norman St Paul's Eccl. Soc. Vol VI, p. 201

H.R. Plomer 3 articles, Home Counties Mag., 1909 & 1910. V. good

St Martin Outwich

Robert Wilkinson Antique Remains from St M.O., 1797. Thin lge 4to, 13 plts inc. 2 plans, 1 interior, 9 plts of monuments and 1 of stained glass

St Mary Abchurch

P. Norman St Paul's Eccl. Soc. Vol VII, p. 99

Rev. R.M. La Porte Payne Short History of St M.A., 1946

E.E.F. Smith Church of St M.A. Ecc. Soc. booklet, 1959

E.E.F. Smith Painted Dome of St M.A. Lon. & Mid. Arch. Soc. booklet, Vol 19, 1958

St Mary Aldermanbury

Pierson C. Carter History of St M.A., 1913. 4to, P.p.

St Mary Aldermary

Rev. H.B. Wilson The Fabric & Glebe of St M.A. Booklet, 1840 – scarce

John Whichcord Article, Lon. & Mid. Arch. Soc. Vol I, 1859

Basil Champneys Article, Portfolio, 1871. P. 124 – on Churches about Queen Victoria Street with real photo

P. Norman Article, St Paul's Eccl. Soc. Vol. VIII, p. 148, *c*.1919

K.S. Mills Article, Ecc. Soc., 1953. p. 85

St Mary-at-Hill

For Churchwardens' Accounts, 1420–1559, see p. 179 (Henry Littlehales)

Parish of St M. at H., its Church Estates & Charities, 1878

P. Norman Article, St Paul's Eccl. Soc. Vol VII, p. 126, *c*.1916

Anon (R.H. Harrison) Article, Ecc. Soc. 1955–56, p. 207. On restorations of 1826 and 1848

St Mary-le-Bow

Geo. Gwilt Article on crypt etc of St M in Vetusta Monumenta Vol V (Soc. of Antiquaries), pp. 1–5. Lge folio with 6 plts inc. dps showing unrestored interior of Wren's church. Valuable

Gents. Mag. 1820, 22, 23 (L. Gomme – Gents. Mag. Lib. – London Vol II)

Rev. A.W. Hutton Short History & Description of Bow Church, Cheapside, 1908

P. Norman St Paul's Eccl. Soc. Vol VII, p. 91, *c*.1913

F. Lambert, W.A. Cater & E.S. Underwood 3 papers on crypt etc, 1915. Illus. and folding plan (Cater reprinted B.A.A. Journal 1917)

St Mary Woolchurch Haw

Sydney Perks History of Mansion House, 1922,

pp. 91–108. See also next item

St Mary Woolnoth

   Rdv. J.M.S. Brooke & A.W.C. Hallen Registers of St M.W. and St M.W.H. with description of churches and extracts of Churchwardens' Accounts & Vestry Minutes. Printed by subscription 1886. Photo of church & 2 plans

   Rev. H.A. Raynes Booklet on St M.W., 1922. On this was based A Brief Account of Church of St M.W. on 200th anniversary of opening in 1727. 8 illus.

   K.S. Mills Article, Ecc. Soc., 1953, p. 93

St Matthew, Friday Street

   Rev. W.S. Simpson Article, Lon. & Mid. Arch. Soc. Vol III, 1870. Notes on History & Antiquities of St M. and St Peter Cheap. (For his Churchwardens' Accounts see p. 179)

St Michael Bassishaw

   P. Norman Archaeologia Vol 58, Pt 1, p. 189. On destroyed church of St Michael, Wood Street . . . with notes on St M.B.

   Chas Welch & F.C. Eeles Lon. & Mid. Arch. Soc. Vol II, 1910, pp. 149–78. Recent discoveries. re. St M.B. etc

   F.C. Eeles Home Counties Mag. Vol I, p. 341. Notes on excavations

   W.B. Passmore Home Counties Mag. Vol II, 1900, pp. 27, 139, 214. History of church and parish

St Michael, Cornhill

   For Churchwardens' Accounts 1456–1608, see p. 179

   P. Norman St Paul's Eccl. Soc. Vol VIII, p. 1, 1917

   Sir E.W. Braybrook Lon. & Mid. Arch. Soc. N.S. Vol IV, 1918–22, p. 376

   K.S. Mills Article, Ecc. Soc., 1950, p. 167

   Anon Church of St M.C. 2 edns – one 1968. Illus.

   W.G. Rogers Woodcarvings in St M.C., c.1870? Many real photos

St Michael, Crooked Lane

   W. Herbert History of St M.C.L., 1831. V. scarce, unfinished, 240 pp. Plt of church

St Michael Paternoster Royal

   P. Norman St Paul's Eccl. Soc. Vol VI, p. 205 Slim booklet, St M.P.R. c.1965. Nice drawings

St Michael Queenhithe

   Robt. Hovenden Copies of Mural Tablets &

Ledger Stones, taken at demolition of church 1876. Sml 8vo. MS 11992 Guildhall Library

St Michael, Wood Street

   Vanishing Landmarks. Article in *Artist*, 1897, p. 384. Half on St M.W.S. with 3 poor drawings

   P. Norman Archaeologia, Vol 58, Pt 1, 1902, p. 189. On destroyed church of St M.W.S. (with St M.B.)

St Mildred, Bread Street

   P. Norman St Paul's Eccl. Soc. Vol VIII, p. 155, c.1920

   Chas Welch Article Lon. & Mid. Arch. Soc. Vol II, 1910. Pp. 149–51. Discovery of Sir Nicholas Crispe's leaden and stone coffins (read 1899)

   Anon Pamphlet on St M.B.S., c.1940

St Mildred Poultry

   T. Milbourne History of St M.P., 1872, 8vo

St Nicholas Cole Abbey

   Rev. J.G.H. Baker 12-page booklet on St N.C.A. 1964

St Olave, Hart Street

   Articles in Gent's Mag., March & April, 1823

   Rev. A. Povah Annals of St O.H.S. & All Hallows Staining, 1894

   G.H. Birch St Paul's Eccl. Soc. Vol I, p. 201, 1881–85

   P. Norman St Paul's Eccl. Soc. Vol V, p. 43, c.1900

   Bryan Corcoran Guide to St O.H.S. 60-page booklet, many illus. 3rd edn 1915

   Rev. T. Wellard A Short Account of St O.H.S. . . . with parishes of All Hallows Staining and St Katherine Coleman, 1927

   Rev. A. Powell Miller 2 booklets: New Annals of St O.H.S., 1954; Short Guide to St O.H.S., c.1956

   E.B. Glanfield (Architect of restoration) Article, Ecc. Soc., 1954

   Booklets of the address at annual Pepys Commemoration Services

St Peter, Cornhill

   R. Wilkinson Article, Londina Illustrata. Lge 4to, 26pp. text, 4 illus.

   P. Norman St Paul's Eccl. Soc. Vol VI, p. 97, c.1907

   K.S. Mills Article, Ecc. Soc., 1950, p. 162

   G. Billam A History of St P-on-C., 1951. Booklet, 4 illus.

St Sepulchre
  Arthur Billing Restoration of St S., Lon., 3rd
    edn, 1884, 8vo. From Builder City Press
  G.J.B. Fox St Paul's Eccl. Soc. Vol IX, 1927
St S. without Newgate
  Rev. G.H. Salter A Watcher at the City Gate for
    48 Reigns. Booklet 1965, named after small bkl
    of 1920. Also St S over against Newgate –
    booklet, 1956; and Some Links with America,
    *c.*1950?
St Stephen, Coleman Street
  See Freshfield's article, Arch. LV, 1887
St Stephen Walbrook
  J.G. White History of Ward of W., 1904, Pp.
    285–399: Church & Parish of St S.W. 8vo
  T. Milbourn St Paul's Eccl. Soc. Vol I, p. 209,
    1885
  P. Norman St Paul's Eccl. Soc. Vol VII, p. 63,
    *c.*1912
  Sydney Perks History of Mansion House, 1922,
    Ch. V, pp. 109–124
  F. & E. Stoneham (Booksellers) Walbrook and
    its Associations, 1925 4to booklet (mostly on
    St S.W.)
  Rev. Chad Varah St S.W., 1955
  J.G. White History of Ward of Walbrook, 1904,
    pp. 403–483
St Swithun, London Stone
  Anon Short History & Guide to St S.L.S., 1934.
    Booklet
St Vedast
  G. Sparrow & W. Sparrow Simpson Life & Legend
    of St V., 1896, 8vo. Deals only with saint,
    except for ch 9 on name of church
  R.C.V. Hodge Church of St V. Foster Lane.
    Pamphlet of little value

Between 1920 and 1939 were issued a monthly series of pamphlets on the City churches: St Erkenwald's Chronicle 1920–32 (4 pp.); and City Chimes 1932–39 (12 pp. & cover). V. rare, only one complete set known to the writer, but the later issues (not so scarce) contain interesting articles on the individual churches and monuments. Mention should also be made of 5 occasional papers (1944–51) of the Friends of the City Churches (founded 1940).

MISCELLANEOUS

CITY CHURCH RELIGIOUS LIFE

James Patterson Pietas Londinensis. 1714, 16mo, on the church services
J. Wickham Legg St Paul's Ecc. Soc. Vol VI, p. 1, 1906. Church services in the reign of Queen Anne: account of the religious societies. (p. 4 the author mis-names these 'Societies for the Reformation of Manners', which were 'for the Suppression of debauchery', not for the advancement of piety.)
H.C. Richards St P's Ecc. Soc. Vol V, *c.*1901, p. 85. John Wesley on London Churches
Rev. Robb Alderson Larner Memorials of St L. Jewry. 1870, sml 8vo. Largely an account of missionary services in St L.J. consequent upon 1st Lambeth Conference 1867
H.W. Clarke The City Churches, 1898. A legalistic and hostile survey of the services (or lack of them) and incumbents' stipends etc – the author recommends demolishing 32 churches and would like to add St Stephen Walbrook!
The London Society The London City Churches, 1923, 2nd edn 1929. 8vo booklet with tabular list of the churches and their present use (by the rectors) and suggestions for their extended use.
Dr J.W.C. Wand, bishop of London. Illus. article in The Sphere, 12 January 1952, pp. 51–57. On the Guild churches scheme.
Isabel M. Calder St Antholin's Lectures, Church Quarterly Review, 1st quarter, 1958, p. 49
D.A. Williams Article, Guildhall Misc., Vol II, 1961, London Puritanism, parish of St Botolph, Aldgate

DEMOLITION OF CITY CHURCHES

Gents. Mag. 1834 and 1854. See Laurence Gomme, Gents. Mag. Library. Top. London, Vol I, 1904, pp. 210–223
In 1853 the Rev. Charles Hume produced a scheme for the demolition of 30 City churches (a copy of the pamphlet is in the Guildhall Library, no. 3114), which eventually led to the passing of the Union of Benefices Act under which many churches have been demolished. See also the Introduction to *Niven*, Churches Destroyed since 1800 (1887), and

Freshfield, Communion Plate of the Churches of the City of London, P.p. 1894.

In 1920 the bishop of London's commission reported in favour of the demolition of 19 City churches (S.P.C.K.) and in 1926 the Union of Benefices and Disposal of Churches Measure was printed (H.M.S.O.).

See also the L.C.C. booklet, Proposed Demolition of 19 City Churches, 1920

Articles in:

The Illustrated London News, 15 May 1920

Country Life, 15 May 1920, Arthur Stratton

Country Life, 13 November 1926, Christopher Hussey

Booklet, Shall All Hallows, Lombard Street be Destroyed?, W.G. Bell and E. Jeffries Davies (City Churches Preservation Society), 1936

History Today, Vol II, 1952, Vanished Churches of the City of London, by Gerald Cobb

CITY CHURCHES IN WARTIME AND AFTER

J. Pope-Hennessy History under Fire, 1941. Sml 4to, 65 illus., 32 of the churches

William Kent Lost Treasures of London, 1947. 7 maps, 47 illus., 23 of City churches and St Clement Danes

Hanslip Fletcher Bombed London, 1947. Thin folio, 37 repros of drawings, 20 of City churches

J.M. Richards & John Summerson Bombed Buildings of Britain, 2nd edn 1947. Many illus., 47 of City churches

Corporation of London A Record of Destruction and Survival, 1951. 4to, nearly 300 illus. (maps, plans, diagrams, pictures), about 50 of the churches

Architectural Press Bombed Churches as War Memorials, 1945, with drawings, plans, photos, mainly of the City

CITY CHURCHYARDS ETC

Henry Carrington Bowles Articles in Gents. Mag., 1824 Pt 1, p. 8, City Churches Burnt 1666 and Not Rebuilt: list with situation and whether burial ground remains. 1827, Pt 1, p. 128, List of tablets recording sites of pre-Fire churches, with their wording

Edw. John Carlos Article in Gents. Mag. 1830, Pt 1, p. 14, on the removal of burying grounds.

These three items, reprinted in Laurence Gomme's Gents. Mag. Library, London, Vol 1 (1904) pp. 208–210 and 224–226

G. Blacker Morgan Catalogue of Tombes, Gravestones...in...Extant Churches of London... by P. Fisher, 1668. Revd & privately reprinted 1885, 100 copies. 4to

P.C. Rushen Churchyard Inscriptions in the City of London, 1910

J.W. Whitlock The City Gardens – Corporation of London 1951, with plan of City and list of churchyards

Mrs. L.B. Ellis Article in B.A.A. Trans., 1943. Boundary and property marks in London – mostly of City parishes

VARIOUS

Parish Clerks' Company New Remarks of London, 1732. Sml 8vo, 410 pp. Brief statistics of each church and parish, personnel etc and lists of streets.

History of London Parishes, 1824 (new edn of above) 156 pp

Charities Endowed Charities of City of London, 1829. 668 pp.

J. Hubbard A...Historical Account of the Parish of All Hallows the Great, 1843. Deals mostly with the charities, 8vo

Rev. A.G. Trower Parish of St Mary-at-Hill, its Estates and Charities, 1878. Monograph, with folding plan of the City after the Fire

Newcourt's Repertorium, 1708, revd and brought up to 1898 by Rev. George Hennessy – Novum Repertorium, 1898, lge 4to. (London Clergy Successions)

Sion College Club for City clergy, founded by Rev. T. White (d. 1623) with fine library. Rev. J. Russell and Rev. Wm. Scott, presidents 1845 and 1858 – Brief Account of Sion College, 1859

VERSES ON CITY CHURCHES

T. Lucey Our City Churches – A few words in rhyme... 2nd edn 1876. Terrible doggerel

J.C. Squire A New Song of the Bishop of London and the City Churches. Ironic verses, decorated by Chris Draper, 1924. 4to

Index